## FIND OUT ALL THE COOL
### MATT FACTS,
#### SUCH AS:

- Matt's dream as a child was to be a professional basketball player
- Matt's first feature-film part was one line in *Mystic Pizza*
- His breakthrough role was as a heroin addict in *Courage Under Fire*, for which he lost 40 pounds
- *Good Will Hunting* is the result of a project he started for his English class at Harvard
- Matt used to breakdance in Harvard Square for money

# MATT DAMON

## KATHLEEN TRACY

St. Martin's Paperbacks

MATT DAMON

Copyright © 1998 by Kathleen Tracy.

Cover photograph by Arnaldo Magnani.

ISBN: 0-312-96857-4

Printed in the United States of America

St. Martin's Paperbacks edition / October 1998

St. Martin's Paperbacks are published by St. Martin's Press, 175 Fifth Avenue, New York, NY 10010.

10  9  8  7  6  5  4  3  2  1

# INTRODUCTION

Hollywood is always looking for the Next Big Thing. It says something about the nature of the entertainment business that the thing in question is actually a person. From the music group Hanson to Leonardo DiCaprio to Matthew McConaughey to the actors on *Ally McBeal*, those concerned with the business part of show business are always desperately seeking the next face that will sell CD-ROMS and movie tickets or attract television viewers by the millions.

More often than not, the Next Big Thing turns out to be a mere Flavor of the Month, quickly replaced by the next new face. Think Anthony Michael Hall. Then there are those who stick around longer, but never live up to the original hype. Think Luke Perry. But on occasion, the Next Big Thing really is. Think Will Smith.

And Matt Damon? Between his blond, teen-idol good looks, his Harvard background, his movie star smile, his shiny new Oscar, and a legion of devoted fans, it seems a good bet that Damon will be one of Hollywood's brightest stars well into the next millennium.

MATT DAMON

**ONE**

**Matt Damon didn't always want to be an actor. And he cer-**
tainly never set out to make his living as a screenwriter.
What he really wanted to be growing up was an athlete.
Specifically, a professional basketball player like his
idol, Nate "Tiny" Archibald, who played for Damon's
beloved Boston Celtics when the Bean Town team won
the NBA title in 1981.

He would watch Archibald on television, driving
down the lane toward the basket or whipping bull's-eye
passes to teammates, then go out and practice those
same moves until his legs and arms ached. While many
kids talk about playing pro ball, Damon obsessed on it
to the point where his father felt the need to deflate his
son's improbable goal, which had begun to take over
much of Matt's waking hours.

"Yeah, I was playing basketball probably seven,
maybe even eight hours a day," Damon recalls. "So one
day when I was twelve, my old man sat me down and
he just said, 'You know, your favorite basketball player,
Tiny Archibald is called "Tiny" because he's 6'1" and
I'm the tallest Damon to ever evolve and I'm 5'1" but
I'm never going to play in the NBA.'

"He made it clear basketball wasn't going to pan out
for me too well. So at twelve, I hung it up. I gave up bas-

ketball and at that moment went into acting, instead. With the same kind of passion. I decided, I'll be an actor and then thought, Can I really do that?"

Damon was brought up in the kind of family where children are raised to believe they can accomplish almost anything and raised in a city, Cambridge, Massachusetts, where creativity and achievement are not only applauded but, to some degree, a civic tradition. Located across the Charles River from Boston, Cambridge is best known as the home of Harvard University, the nation's oldest college, the Massachusetts Institute of Technology, and several other smaller, but prestigious, colleges.

Cambridge, which was originally settled by the Puritans back in 1630, has built up around several major squares, or plazas, each with its own unique personality. Harvard Square, for example, is a center of activity at any time of day year-round. Performers juggle, mime, sing, and play their instruments to the entertainment of the passersby. Located near the university, the area is filled with shops, restaurants, and theaters and in the open air plaza, chess players compete in silent concentration, oblivious to the swirl of activity around them.

"I grew up in Central Square, which is kind of between Harvard and MIT," explains Damon. "So my upbringing was middle-class in a multicultural neighborhood that was working class. It's a great way for an actor to grow up because you're sitting there watching people all the time who are totally different, from different class systems."

Despite being just across the river from the Boston metropolis, Cambridge has remained small and somewhat insular, with under 100,000 full-time residents.

"Cambridge is not that big of a place. It's more like

the People's Republic of Cambridge," Damon wryly notes, referring to the cliquey nature of the town, which is often divided between those affiliated with the academic community, as either students or employees, and those who aren't.

"In Central, we are proprietary about our city. We kind of view Harvard students in a different light. I always had an underdog complex growing up, even on a subconscious level."

But besides growing up in the ever-present glare of the town's academic superstars, Matt had other reasons to feel insecure as a child. Born October 8, 1970, Matt was the youngest of two sons, his brother Kyle being three years older. When he was two, Matt's parents divorced.

"My dad had this *Leave It to Beaver* idea of how life should be and it just didn't work out," is how Matt explains the breakup

Kent Damon has been described variously as a tax preparer, tax expert, financial analyst, realtor, and stockbroker. According to Matt, his father, who has since retired, worked in real estate, specializing in raising corporate funds for low-income housing.

"But now Dad is the baseball coach for the freshman high school team in a neighboring town," Matt says with a smile.

Despite the divorce, Kent and Matt's mother, Nancy Carlsson-Paige, maintained an amicable relationship. So much so that years later, they celebrated what would have been their twenty-fifth wedding anniversary.

"My dad took my mom, Kyle, and me out to dinner," remembers Matt. "And he's like, 'This is great. The nuclear family is finally together again.' When the waiter asks if we'd like some wine, Dad goes, 'Of course! It's our twenty-fifth anniversary.' But the waiter announces it to the whole restaurant, so Dad has to say,

'Wait, wait. We've been divorced for nineteen of those years.' The whole place went silent. Oh, it was good."

Although Kent remained actively involved with Matt and Kyle's upbringing, the two boys spent most of their time with their mother, who is a professor of early childhood development at Lesley College, a small teacher's college located near Harvard. And because of her area of expertise, Nancy had some definite ideas about how children should, and should not, be raised. She particularly disapproved of war toys and what she considered the inherent violence of cartoons.

"My mother had written some books on war play and those cartoons that are like commercials for action figures," Matt explains. "What worried my mother about these shows was not only that they encouraged violent play but that they also hampered creativity."

So, unlike most children born in the past fifty years, Damon didn't grow up with an arsenal of toy guns. Nor did television play a pivotal role in Matt's early development. Although many younger actors and entertainers, such as Jerry Seinfeld and Drew Carey, freely admit they were couch potatoes long before the phrase was coined, Damon's mother insisted her children learn to amuse themselves, rather than let the TV do it for them. As a result, Matt was forced to use his imagination for fun, which often led to playacting.

"Growing up for me was like you'd get some blocks and then you'd have to make up a game. In our house, we only had blocks to play with. My brother and I hated these blocks. But Kyle would make these really amazing costumes which I'd wear and we'd act out these stories. And that was really cool. I used to think I was a superhero and I'd dress up as superheroes."

"He wore a superhero towel around his neck day in and day out for a couple of years," confirms his mom.

But sometimes Matt got carried away with his flair for the dramatic.

"I really did stupid stuff when I was a little kid," he admits. "Like when I was four years old and thought I was Shazam. Shazam got his power by screaming '*Shazam!*' Then he'd be able to fly. So I climbed to the top of the jungle gym and I had a little blue towel around my neck and I screamed '*Shazam!*' and jumped. But I didn't fly. I went straight down and that was it for me. I broke my ankle."

With due deference to Damon, Shazam wasn't the name of a character. It was the word used by comic book character Billy Batson to turn himself into Captain Marvel, the World's Mightiest Mortal. Shazam was an acronym for the six immortal elders—Solomon, Hercules, Atlas, Zeus, Achilles, and Mercury—who, according to the comic, had given Billy his powers. But considering Matt was only four at the time, his memory lapse should be forgiven.

However sketchy the details are of his brief career as a superhero, one vivid memory remains.

"I think my desire to become an actor may have started there." Matt says.

But it would be several years before Damon would begin to seriously pursue that interest. In the meantime, the young boy with the blond, tousled hair was the picture of the All-American boy, espcially when playing the All-American sport in Little League. His baseball hero was hometown legend, Boston Red Sox Hall of Fame catcher, Carlton Fisk.

"I had a Carlton Fisk uniform when I was a little kid, and I wore his number, 27, in Little League," Damon recalls.

Because he was so young when his parents split up, Matt didn't suffer any particular emotional fallout over it and remembers his childhood fondly. In the winter, Cambridge looked like a postcard, with the snow glistening off the spires of the nearby universities. When it wasn't too cold, Matt would go sledding, but most of the winter was spent indoors passing the time reading or just hanging out with his brother, Kyle.

During the summer, however, Matt spent most of his time outdoors, practicing his basketball moves, playing baseball, riding his bike, and mingling with the tourists who take day trips to Cambridge, which has a rich and varied history separate and distinct from Boston.

The city was founded in 1630, after a fleet of eleven ships carrying 700 Puritan passengers, arrived at the Massachusetts Bay Colony. The newcomers established several villages around Massachusetts Bay, but couldn't agree on a capital. Wanting a protected area, John Winthrop chose a small hill on the north bank of the Charles River, five miles upstream from Boston and named the settlement Newtowne, which was changed to Cambridge in 1638.

For centuries, Cambridge was a mostly rural area, but in more recent times, it has become a bedroom suburb for Boston's ever-growing population. As a result, during the time Damon was growing up, Cambridge was undergoing its own growing pains, with an escalating population squeezing out some of the town's quaint charm. But for the local kids, demographics and increased congestion were issues for the academic types that populated Harvard Square. Matt's world revolved around his own neighborhood, his family, and his friends. Especially one friend in particular.

Matt Damon's life story is so intertwined with that of his childhood friend, Ben Affleck, that it would be impossible to separate the two. While most kids have a best friend who they are inseparable from for a period of time, Matt and Ben never grew apart; they simply grew closer the older they got. Their relationship was, and still is, as close as brothers without the familial rivalry. They were soul mates before they even knew what the word meant. And they might have never been friends if it weren't for the insistence of their mothers, who were both teachers, although Mrs. Affleck taught elementary school.

Matt was ten and Ben was eight, when they were first introduced and it wasn't exactly like at first sight.

"I was pretty much forced into hanging out with Ben," Matt laughs. "I remember exactly what Ben was like as a kid: gregarious and outgoing. Except when he used to ring my bell then cower on the other side of the street because he was afraid of the little kids at the school next door to my house. But believe me, it's no surprise that he grew into the totally obnoxious guy he is now."

Although the two youngsters didn't think they had much in common at first, they soon discovered mutual ground: both were interested in acting, although they had been introduced to performing in quite different ways.

"I grew up just always making up stories and acting out plays," Matt comments. "That's just the way I was raised. But Ben came from a more prestigious background."

Affleck's father, who helped rehabilitate alcoholics and drug addicts in his day job, had worked in a theater company in Boston for a long time, so Ben had grown up with access to a performing atmosphere, watching actors up close.

Damon's interest had initially developed out of the sheer joy he experienced in his playacting. About a year or so prior to meeting Ben, Matt had finally started to pursue his interest in acting more avidly.

"When I was eight or nine, I started getting into children's theater groups," he recalls. "My parents agreed that if I were interested in it, it was fine but they weren't stage parents or anything.

"My mom and dad thought being in theater workshops with other little kids was a healthy thing. I also still played Little League and other stuff too—in fact, I was the best pitcher in the League—but acting was something I always wanted to do and they kept encouraging me to do it, really to do whatever I wanted. That was their theory: Just be happy."

When Matt and Ben met, Affleck was already a neighborhood celebrity, having been hired to host a PBS children's show called *Voyage of the Mimi*. It was a series designed to interest youngsters in marine life and was filmed aboard the *Mimi* of the Maine seacoast. The ship's skipper was Clement Granville, and had a crew of three teenagers. Affleck would go on to host the show for six years, until he was fourteen.

Suddenly, Ben became the kid everyone looked up to. Somewhat surprisingly, since Matt aspired to the same goals, Affleck's success didn't arouse envy in Matt. Instead, it made him feel vindicated.

"Ben was the movie star of our block," says Damon. "Ben was like the biggest star in Cambridge, Massachusetts, and he was *my* best friend. I was the theater kid and he was the television kid."

As far as Ben was concerned, he was just one of the lucky kids who was getting to do a really fun job.

"Acting for me was more like, 'You know, I really kind of like this. This is fun.' It was just something that was really pleasant and when you're young, it's about being comfortable."

Suddenly, even though Ben was two years younger, he

became the resident expert on all things acting and Matt looked to him for guidance and information.

"Of course I thought he knew everything because he'd done the PBS show," Damon acknowledges. "And we had done a TJ Maxx commercial together and had gotten paid $200 bucks apiece which was the money I used to go to New York and get back. So yeah, he was the guy."

Having found a captive audience in each other, Ben and Matt would play theater games and put on plays together, feeding off one another's ideas, oblivious to anyone else who might not appreciate their passion for performing.

"It was kind of nerdy, actually," admits Ben now of their interest in being actors. "People would look at us like, 'Why don't you wanna be a fireman like a normal kid?' "

"I think we just look at the world in the same way," Damon notes. "Ben's the funniest guy I know and I just admire him greatly. You gotta admire a close friend of yours."

"It's like any friendship someone's had since they were little," adds Affleck. "It's not like we're the Wonder Twins or anything. We were just lucky enough to want to do the same thing."

"We did everything together," says Damon. "From Little League to chasing girls but from a very early age, what we focused on the most was acting."

# TWO

**Once their friendship was forged, Matt and Ben quickly** became inseparable. Matt's house was only two blocks from Ben and they attended the same grammar school so the boys often walked to school together, despite the two-year age difference.

"We grew up in the same neighborhood, playing the same games and experiencing the same things," Damon says. "If one of us had enough money for a candy bar, then the candy bar was bought and split in half. That's just the way it's always been."

Although their mothers were both teachers, Affleck notes that their families' bond went deeper than a shared profession.

"People of similar political persuasions tend to flock together," he says, "and most lefties in Cambridge County know each other."

And Nancy Carlsson-Paige made no bones about her liberal political and social leanings and didn't hesitate to apply them to her life and the lives of her children. For example, his mother's longtime boyfriend, who had driven one of the buses that drove black kids to white schools in "Southie" in the mid-seventies, would take Matt on tours of South Boston, giving the youngster lessons in race relations.

In fact, Damon's upbringing stuck out as considerably liberal even in such a well-known liberal area. The most vivid example of his mother's commitment to social consciousness and determination to live her beliefs was when she and her sons moved into an experimental cooperative house or "community house" when Matt was ten, around the same time he and Ben became friends.

"About six families bought a broken-down house in central Square and rebuilt it," Damon explains. "It was governed by a shared philosophy that housing is a basic human right. Every week there was a three-hour community meeting and Sundays were workdays. I remember my mom put little masks on me and my brother, gave us goggles and crowbars, and we'd demolish the walls."

While most adults would be uncomfortable in such a dormitory-style living situation, for the kids of the community house, the more was definitely the merrier.

"Everyone had their own apartment, but the kids felt free to wander," recalls Matt. "Everyone had their space and as a kid it was heaven. If your mom was out or not in the mood for you, there was always another mother around who was.

"That was during pretty formative years, junior high and high school, and it was a great way to be raised, especially for an actor. You were exposed to lots of different perspectives and were just surrounded by lots of positive human beings."

Ben, who was there so much he became an unofficial member of the house, says the community house wasn't as extreme as it may sound to some.

"You say *commune* and you start to think of some off-in-the-wilderness, barefoot, and bell-bottoms, sort of flaky hippie living. But this was a much more practical arrangement."

"Actually," smiles Damon, "you *could* call them hippies. They had all the same views on money and politics, raising children."

Then he adds gently, with a smile: "My mom is a very radical lady."

For two boys from a broken home, the community house added a sense of stability for Matt and his brother Kyle. Although their father Kent may not have been around all the time to keep his eye on the boys, there were plenty of other adults around to make sure the Damon brothers stayed on the straight and narrow.

"Being the youngest brother of two, I've gotten my ass kicked my entire life," Matt laughs. "And it hasn't stopped. Even now at twenty-seven, I still don't think I could ever get away with misbehaving."

Kyle agrees. "We didn't rebel much. We didn't do drugs, stay out late or bad-mouth our parents."

Damon also believes their communal living arrangement fostered creativity, because the children were encouraged to experiment and not be afraid to try different things. Which in Matt's case meant occasionally break dancing in Harvard Square for extra money.

"Kyle turned out to be a sculptor and an artist and I turned out to be an actor," Damon points out. "I think our paths were clearly defined at a really early age."

But there were still some situations that the community house couldn't mask for the children of divorce, especially around the holidays.

"Because I come from a family of divorced parents and remarried parents, it's a pretty wacky family," Matt says mildly. "So Christmases were always kinds of time of being pulled in every single direction. Because of that, it's not really about sitting there enjoying your time together, it's like looking at your watch the whole time because you have to drive two hours to get to the next place.

"That's why I'd say the biggest Christmas memory I have happened when I was older. My brother, who by that time was married with a wife whose family was like ours, walked into my mother's house one year and he had circles under his eyes he was so tired from running around from house to house. He just looked at everybody and said, 'Christmas is at my house next year and anyone who wants to come is invited, if not, it's too bad; you're spending Christmas alone.' And we did. Because of him, the next year everyone got together and it was just terrific."

When Matt was twelve, after his basketball aspirations had been subverted, he graduated from theater groups to performing in actual theater productions. He also studied pantomime and took other classes he believed would prepare him for an acting career. And while television was still not an influence in his life, the movies shown on it were. He would spend hours watching movies and studying the acting styles of idols like Robert Duvall and Robert DeNiro.

"Then when he was fourteen and I was sixteen, [Ben] came up to me, in his infinite wisdom, he'd seen me act all through high school, and said, 'I can get you an audition,' with his agent in New York. So I announced to my mom and dad that I was ready to go pro, as if I were a baseball player. They were just baffled," Matt laughs.

Matt and Ben plotted the trip to New York down to the last detail.

"This trip was a big deal. We figured out my wardrobe. I had my Syracuse Orangemen sweatshirt on, and I knew *everything*. So Ben and I took the train to New York and he introduced me to his agent.

"So I walked into the office with all this confidence, and here we were the two chumpiest kids in the world. It was like this Mom and Pop agency and they didn't even know who Ben was. But Ben thought he was the biggest star in the world and he's going, 'This is Matt. He's an actor too.'

"And I'm kind of too cool to talk. They looked at me and said, 'Yeah, we'll represent Matt too.' And I never got a phone call from them.

"But what was great about it was that I thought I had an agent. I ended up doing really well in high school and I went to Harvard because I figured my career is being taken care of. It just takes a little time.

"Eventually, when I was eighteen, I traded up and got a better agent who actually got me auditions, which was a nice change. And by my sophomore year in college, I was auditioning for things, but all of that only came about because I was confident that I had an agent handling my career for me for all those years."

When Matt was sixteen, he enrolled at the prestigious Cambridge Rindge and Latin High School, which is located right next door to Harvard.

"I think the mayor sweeps a few of us in under the carpet," jokes Damon, referring to his family's lack of social standing. And indeed, the school has some famous alumni, including poet e. e. cummings, *Doogie Howser* co-star Max Casella and New York Knicks star Patrick Ewing. It also has educated the infamous, as in the case of Gina Grant. Grant, a straight-A student with an IQ of 150, made headlines in 1995 when Harvard rescinded its acceptance offer after learning Gina had served time in a juvenile facility for killing her mother four years earlier. She attended Tufts University instead.

Despite his tendency to downplay his intelligence and academic abilities, Damon was a good student. He was also popular, with his shock of blond hair and surfer-boy good looks.

Ben's younger brother Casey, recalls Matt as a local teen idol long before the rest of America caught on.

"In high school, Matt was the guy who always sat in the back of the bus making out with his girlfriends."

In fact, Matt's interest in girls had started long before high school.

"I remember the first movie where I made out with a girl," Damon says. "It was *48 Hours* with Nick Nolte and Eddie Murphy. It was an R-rated movie and I was really afraid I wouldn't get in because I was only twelve. But I did and it was so cool."

Despite his popularity with the young ladies Matt spent most of his free time with Ben. They would go hang out at the local video arcade called One Thousand and One Plays and afterward usually go buy a slice of pizza as a late night snack on their way home.

When he was old enough, Ben followed Matt to Cambridge Rindge and Latin, which had a particularly strong drama program that put on productions not typical for most high schools. For example, Matt's first stage appearance was playing a saurai in a Kabuki play.

"I had an amazing drama teacher in high school named Gary Speca and Ben and I owe everything to him."

Speca remembers his former student fondly. "Matt was this little dervish, running around, rehearsing his part, all his moves, making sure everything was just right."

But whereas Matt was a solid overall student, Ben was less apt to apply himself to subjects he was less interested in. He was the classic example of a student who doesn't live up to his potential.

"Matt was an ambitious student in a mediocre program," Affleck explains. "I was an unambitious student in a difficult program—excuse me, pilot program."

Ben goes on to chide Matt about his tendency to go out of his way to charm his instructors.

"Matt was the kind of guy who brought in a lot of apples to his teachers, if you see what I'm getting at. I was a little more contentious, with a habit of challenging my teachers."

Damon, though, always seemed to be in the thick of things, enthusiastically participating in school activities, such as volunteering to perform the song "Burning Down the House" at one of the talent shows. He was outgoing and friendly and felt comfortable with his social, athletic, and academic abilities.

But Matt and Ben's disparate personalities complimented one another and their friendship continued to strengthen through their teen years and they continued to spend the majority of their time together. Naturally, once he got his driver's license, Affleck would pick Damon up for school in his very uncool Toyota Corona. It should be noted that Damon is often the butt of jokes about his less-than-sure driving skills, which is why Affleck was the one behind the wheel.

Hardly a day went by that Matt and Ben didn't fortify their dreams by reaffirming their commitment to "making it." As teenagers, it became a tradition for the friends to meet in the smaller of the high school's two cafeterias, ironically called the Media Cafeteria.

"Ben and I used to have what we called business lunches, which meant we met at a different cafeteria from everyone else. We would take our cheeseburgers and sit down at a table in the Media caf and we would talk business. Even though there was nothing to talk about!"

Mostly, they would talk about their plans to conquer Hollywood when they were older.

"We'd sit there with our little crappy fifty-cent chicken sandwiches and say things like, 'We're going to be big actors. We're going to take the town by storm!' " Affleck says.

Damon laughs at the memory. "Yeah, we'd say things like, 'We're going to be huge. We're going to be the biggest actors. Okay, so how was Spanish class today?' "

"We were really nerdy," Ben says, shaking his head.

When Matt's obsession with acting didn't go the way of his basketball dreams, Nancy and Kent realized just how serious their son was about pursuing it as a career. Although his parents were supportive, they did make sure he understood what a difficult profession it was.

"They advised me that acting was a brutal profession," recalls Matt. "They told me, 'People are going to lie to you, take advantage of you and there aren't going to be any jobs for you.' But they never told me I couldn't act."

Damon's mom, in particular, though, wasn't shy about expressing her reservations about acting, particularly since in her eyes it lacked any social consciousness.

"I was talking to my mother one day, when I was sixteen or seventeen, and she goes, 'Matt, why are you so obsessed with acting?'

"And I tried to explain it to her. That whatever I did, I wanted to be the best at. I remember that moment in *The Natural* when Robert Redford says, 'There goes Roy Hobbs, the best there ever was.' So I said to her, 'Because some day I want to walk down the street and have people say, "There goes Matt Damon, the best there ever was.' "

"And she said, 'Did I raise you? That's just an egomaniacal pipe dream. How does it help other people?' Of course, I hadn't given much thought to that."

Seeing how unenthusiastic Matt's mom was about their acting dreams, Ben tried to help smooth things over with Nancy.

"I remember being in high school and trying to convince Matt's mother that not everybody in Hollywood was a total liar or scum," laughs Affleck. "I told her there are people in Hollywood who have a social consciousness, too. I only repeat this because years later, I now I realize it was a complete lie."

Chris Affleck, Ben's mother, was more gentle in her skepticism, although neither she nor her husband wanted their son to pursue acting as a career.

"Every time we sat down for dinner, Chris would say, 'Why don't you boys become doctors?' " recalls Ben. "I think our parents were concerned because everybody knows that acting is a difficult career. I don't think they were happy with the prospect of their kids facing a lifetime of rejection and scraping by for a sandwich and hoping we'd get free refills at age forty-five.

"But Matt and I were very straightforward about wanting to be actors. I really think that everybody wants to be an actor. Why wouldn't they? It's great work if you can get it. The one thing that prevents most people from saying 'I'm just gonna go to Hollywood,' is that it seems unrealistic."

But it seemed very attainable to Matt, especially after appearing in his very first movie when he was seventeen. Damon had one line in the film *Mystic Pizza*, which was shot in the Boston area.

*"Mom, do you want my green stuff?"*

The film told the story of two sisters and their search for love. Although a modest success, the movie's biggest claim to fame was that it launched the career of Julia Roberts.

"I was a little high school kid and I got to say one line. Julia Roberts sat across from me at a dinner table and I remember thinking she was beautiful, but she wasn't 'Julia Roberts' yet. I was so excited and my mother was sitting behind the camera with a big grin on her face."

Proving that even liberal-minded professors filled with skepticism toward Hollywood are still, first and foremost, proud parents.

Matt also worked as an extra on *The Good Mother*. The movie starred Diane Keaton as a woman who becomes embroiled in a custody battle with her ex-husband over their daughter. And although the movie itself was humorless and dreary, for Matt is was a thrill ride to be on the same set with Keaton and her co-star, a then relatively unknown Liam Neeson.

As Matt's senior year drew to a close, his future seemed rosy. He had been accepted into Harvard and was looking forward to continuing his education while patiently waiting for his agent in New York to guide him into a career. The only blemish on an otherwise golden high school experience occurred shortly before graduation, during his senior prom, proving that even heartthrobs can have their hearts broken.

Matt's date for what was supposed to the most romantic of high school nights was named Tammy Jones. Tall and gorgeous, Tammy was on the school basketball team and towered over the diminutive Damon by almost six inches. Even so, he was absolutely smitten with her.

"I thought she was really pretty and I was hopelessly in love with her—and it turned into the worst date I ever had," Damon admits. "Tammy hooked up with another guy, while I was in the room. I mean I was heartbroken, crestfallen, and cried myself to sleep."

Damon pauses a moment, then shakes off the painful memory with a shrug and the perspective of a young man whose romantic horizons have expanded exponentially.

"Now, though," he says casually, "there are a lot of other girls who I would take to the prom before her."

And there are a lot of girls who would be lining up to go.

# THREE

**Some would-be actors feel such an urgency to start a career** that they bypass college and head straight to New York or L.A. before the ink is even dry on their high school diplomas. Damon, on the other hand, didn't suffer from that kind of anxious restlessness. He was so confident he would indeed eventually have an acting career, Matt was able to go off to college and actually enjoy the experience. He wasn't preoccupied with worries that he was missing out on opportunities so he could concentrate on what Harvard had to offer him.

Ironically, although he was accepted at Harvard, Matt had originally wanted to attend Yale, which has a well-known drama department and boasts alumni including Jodie Foster, Brooke Shields, and Christopher Reeve. Harvard's drama department is less noted, but still prestigious, and Damon does believe he was lucky to meet the teachers he did.

"There's an acting teacher at Harvard named David Wheeler who I think is the best acting teacher in the country," Damon says resolutely. "Al Pacino goes to him every time before he plays a role to talk to him about it. David teaches a class called 'Introduction to Acting' for undergraduates and he got his hands on me when I was seventeen. I took every class that he offered and he placed me in a couple of plays. He's just extra-ordinary."

Damon downplays his own academic prowess when talking about gaining admittance to one of the nation's most difficult schools to get in.

"Oh, I think they just swept some of us in," he laughs, then adds seriously. "They saw that I was dedicated to something and that I tried hard at it. The opening line in the essay for my application to Harvard was, *'For as long as I can remember, I've wanted to be an actor.'* "

For Matt, who declared English as his major, college was a gold mine because it gave him a chance to immerse himself in an environment dedicated solely to improving one's horizons. He wasn't just interested in being an actor, he was a student of acting. Even though he might have possessed an innate desire to perform and some inherent talent, he knew he needed to learn as much as he could about the craft of acting if he was ever going to measure up to his idols.

But for Damon, learning meant more than just hitting the books, listening to a professor expound, or turning in writing assignments. It also meant studying the very people whose work he admired.

"I look at acting kind of as a trade," he says. "The only way to get better was to apprentice yourself to the masters. I think the masters of today are in films—people like Robert Duvall, Denzel Washington, Mickey Rourke, Jon Voight, Francis McDormand, and Robin Williams—and I just like to watch them. I feel like I grow exponentially when I watch them.

"I think the best actor in the country is Morgan Freeman. He and Robert Duvall. It comes with their age and experience. They can make things happen without doing much.

"I hope in fifty years acting still makes me excited. I look at Jon Voight, who's so enthusiastic, and I hope I can be like that."

Damon believes there's a great difference between actors of the past generation and those now, insofar as many of the younger generation don't seem as willing to put in the work necessary to be a great actor, as opposed to a movie star. Ironically, he blames the man many still believe is one of America's greatest actors for this trend.

"I think Marlon Brando has done more to destroy this generation of actors with this whole marble-mouth thing and the I-don't-give-a-f--- mentality," Damon says. "What people overlook is that when the dude was my age, he was the hardest working man in show business. He had a discipline that was unmatched. He was onstage, he was busting his ass with Stella Adler, he was *obsessed* with acting.

"But now, because he gets away with everything. The younger guys are like, 'Oh, all I gotta do is get fat and go to Fiji and have everybody tell me I'm a genius.' I mean, that's just not true. They're not looking at what it actually takes to get there."

To understand Matt, one has to appreciate that despite being raised in a family with a white-collar background, Damon grew up instilled with a blue-collar work ethic, no doubt in large part provided by his youthful experiences as part of the community home. Matt believed that only through hard work would he ever fulfill his dream to be an actor. And the people he admired most were the ones who worked the hardest.

"Robert Duvall, for example, is still like that," Damon enthuses. "That's why I think Duval is such an *amazing* actor. He's in his fifties and he's still doing it. I hope that the ethic hasn't been lost, because that's what defined actors and made acting great in America. We had these great teachers and these students who busted their asses. I think there are still some good guys out there."

And he was determined to be one of them. Although the road to respectability would be paved with more than a few indignities and humbling experiences along the way. Such as the time Matt wrongly thought he was meeting the head of a studio.

"This is a horrible, embarrassing story. I was going with Ben to New York to meet Ben's agent, who had arranged an audition for me. This was probably the third 'meeting' I'd had in two years and I told everyone I was going to New York to meet the president of Walt Disney.

"So I go to New York but it turns out I'm not meeting the president—it's just an audition for *The Mickey Mouse Club*, complete with ears. Then I had to go back to school and everyone was asking how the audition went. To this day, Ben and I still talk about that.

"And I didn't even get the job either," Matt laughs.

Despite his dedication to his studies and to acting, Damon didn't skimp on enjoying the social aspects of college. Even though Cambridge was his home, Matt lived in a dorm at the college, and during his free time, he and his newfound buddies could often be found hanging out at Harvard Square's Bow and Arrow Pub.

He also kept in constant contact with his family and with Ben, who was still attending high school. His experience of traveling back and forth between the two worlds would have an important impact on Matt. Because he grew up a "local," Damon knew what it was like to feel the part of the underdog. Many kids growing up in the reflected glare of Harvard's glittering student body felt insecure and perhaps a little inferior. Matt himself has admitted to feeling that way.

Part of it is Harvard's storied history. Established in 1636 as a ministry school, it was named after John Harvard, a Charleston minister. When Harvard died in 1638, he left his entire estate to the new institution. In return, the institution adopted the minister's name.

Currently, the university employs over 2,000 educators and boasts 17,000 full-time undergraduate and graduate students—at a cost in excess of $25,000 per year. In its over 350-year history, Harvard has been home to thirty-five Nobel laureates and scores of prominent people in government, business, and law.

Once Damon was inside those ivy-covered walls of Harvard, however, he realized that admittance to the university didn't guarantee a life of success and achievement. All it did was give you an opportunity to reach whatever potential you had. Matt's underdog insecurity, and his desire to succeed as an actor, meant that he would work twice as hard to prove that he indeed belonged at Harvard with the others there.

As it turned out, Damon's college experience was destined to be continually interrupted by acting work. Once Matt had wised up that the agent Ben set him up with when he was sixteen was not actively trying to secure him auditions, Damon signed with a different representative who did.

And suddenly, he found himself being hired. It didn't matter to Damon how big the part was or if it was in cable movies, which at that time had yet to gain the prestige they have now. All Matt wanted to do was work because it was the best way to learn to be a better actor.

"I started working when I was nineteen. It was a project on cable for TNT, Turner Network Television, called *Rising Son*. I got hired for that when I was in the second semester of my sophomore year."

Which meant that Matt had to withdraw from school

for the term in order to go make the film, in which Matt played the son of Brian Dennehy and Piper Laurie. *Rising Son* told the story of a middle-aged man struggling to deal with the loss of his job as well as his troubled relationship with his teenage son.

Dennehy played Gus Robinson, a foreman in a Detroit auto factory. The conflict is set up when his youngest son, Charlie, comes home from college one weekend and announces that he has dropped out of his premed studies because he doesn't want to be a doctor. Instead, he wants to work on the same assembly line as his father. So when the plant starts laying off employees, Gus is not only worried about his own future, but Charlie's as well.

The movie first aired Monday, July 23, 1990. Although Damon's role was pivotal, the film was primarily a showcase for Dennehy and reviews of the movie were generally positive.

"No actor is physically better-suited to play this sort of sensitive blue-collar man than beefy Brian Dennehy," noted *Entertainment Weekly* television critic Ken Tucker.

"Equally good are the explosive scenes between Dennehy and Damon (rarely has a father-son quarrel been as frank) and the quiet scenes between Dennehy and Piper Laurie as his wife. Subtle and moving, *Rising Son* is a job well done by all."

*People* magazine's critic, David Hiltbrand, was less enamored with the movie as a whole, but singled out the performances.

"In a poignant film reminiscent of the work of playwright Jason Miller, Brian Dennehy plays a man swamped by disappointment," Hiltbrand wrote. "The Pennsylvania factory he had worked at all his adult life has just closed, and the younger son on whom he had pinned great hopes announces he has dropped out of his premed program.

"The drama is overdone at times, particularly when it tries to make points about the decline of American industry. But affecting performances by Dennehy, Damon, and Piper Laurie, as the lady of the house, keep this film from getting far off the track."

In addition to giving Matt his first reviews, *Rising Son* was also Damon's first exposure to working with other experienced actors of substance. And he rose to the occasion. Brian Dennehy remembers his TV son as someone who, while maybe still a little green, had all the right tools to work with.

"He's a bright, smart, sensitive kid," Dennehy says. "And he's hardworking. But he's got one thing that's rare and important—he's disciplined. He has controls, brakes, and that's unusual. We're all familiar with the James Dean wanna-be's and that's definitely *not* where Matt's at. His self-control makes him different in a town that sometimes rewards you for bad behavior.

"He's also a pleasant guy, one of those guys who can get along with anybody, the crew, everyone."

Matt rode his emotional high back to Harvard, and picked up his studies where he had left off while waiting for the next role he felt was sure to come. *Rising Son* had put him on the radar screen and Damon knew it was just a matter of time before the next job came his way. Again, that confidence allowed him to concentrate on his schoolwork rather than being preoccupied with worries over whether he would ever get another acting job again.

And Damon had other things on his mind besides writing assignments and acting auditions because Matt was in love. The object of his affections was a beautiful Columbia University medical student named Skylar

Satenstein. Because Skylar lived in New York City, Matt would travel into Manhattan every chance he got in order to spend time with her.

One of their favorite places to go was Tom's Restaurant, the diner whose exterior was featured on *Seinfeld*, and made famous as "Monk's." Tom's was in the same Upper Westside neighborhood where Skylar lived and Matt loved going into the diner to order grilled-cheese sandwiches. Although Matt and Skylar lived apart and didn't see each other on a daily basis, the relationship was a serious one and Matt was convinced she was the woman he wanted to spend the rest of his life with.

Life was good and Damon felt good about himself— and was about to feel even better. In the second semester of Matt's junior year, he was cast in the movie, *School Ties*, which was produced by Sherry Lansing, who also had a hand in the casting. It would be his first feature film role of consequence, in which Damon played a moneyed legacy student whose anti-Semitism and resentment of a Jewish student propels the film's action. It would also introduce Matt to a group of peers with whom he would develop lasting ties of his own.

Damon was naturally excited at the prospect of doing a film but he was forced to put his enthusiasm on hold when the production was delayed.

"I had already withdrawn for the semester when *School Ties* suddenly got postponed," Matt recalls. "So I lost that semester but we finally did the movie the following fall, in what *would* have been my senior year."

*School Ties* was following on the wave created by the success of the surprise hit *Dead Poet's Society*, which starred Robin Williams as an inspirational teacher and put the phrase *carpe diem* ("seize the day") into the general vernacular.

Just like *Dead Poet's Society*, *School Ties* had a cast

of unknown up-and-comers, including Brendan Fraser in the lead role, Chris O'Donnell, Randall Batinkoff, and Cole Hauser in supporting parts. But the best casting news for Matt was that Ben had also been cast for a role. By this time, Affleck had graduated from high school. He had attended Occidental College but dropped out in 1991 to pursue acting full-time.

"I realized there were other things I'd rather do with $20,000 a year," Ben quips.

So *School Ties* gave the two buddies a chance to work together and rekindle their long-held dreams. The movie was filmed on location all around the Boston area. Set in the 1950s, the story centered around a Jewish kid, David Greene, who wins a scholarship to a WASPy prep school in New England. The school alumni are so desperate for a winning season, they will do anything—even recruit a Jew.

For his part, Greene sees the prep school as a stepping stone into one of the prestigious Ivy League schools. Although the school officials are aware of Greene's cultural background, the students don't so David decides to keep the fact he is Jewish a secret. Even if it means playing football on an important holy day such as Rosh Hashanah and ignoring derogatory remarks about Jews casually made by some of his classmates.

At first David seems to be fitting in with the other students, most of them the sons of privilege who are under constant pressure to keep up the family name. Damon played one such scion, named Charlie Dillon. Charlie is resentful of both David, who replaced him as the starting quarterback, and the fact that he feels he's trapped in a no-win situation. If he fails to live up to expectations, he'll let the family down, but even if he succeeds, people will think it's only because of family connections.

David's secret, though, is revealed when one of the alumni gets drunk and reveals the truth about Greene's background. All of a sudden, David becomes the object of scorn. He's the butt of ugly jokes, he finds a swastika painted on the door of his room and he has a fight with Charlie. And his roommate and friend, Chris Reece, played by Chris O'Donnell, is angry with him for not sharing his true identity with him.

Eventually, the other students have to confront their anti-Semitism and the movie becomes a lesson about prejudice. Film critic Roger Ebert gave the film a thumbs-up.

"*School Ties* is surprisingly effective. It is not simply about anti-Semitism, but also about the way that bigotry can do harm by inspiring dishonesty. One of David's friends tells him it would have been best for him to proudly proclaim his Jewishness on the first day of school, and of course that is right; to remain secretive is to grant the bigots the power of their hate.

"Brendan Fraser, whose previous performance was as the thawed-out prehistoric *Encino Man* is crucial to this movie's success. His performance has to find the way between his character's ambition and pride; he knows that this prep school is the only possible route for him between working-class Scranton and a scholarship to Harvard, and he doesn't want to lose his chance. But at the expense of tradition? By the end of the movie, he knows the answer to that question."

When the movie opened in 1992, it was a thrilling time for Matt. His family was justifiably proud, his college buddies were teasing him about being a big movie star, and Damon was pleased to show Skylar that he really was going to make it as an actor.

Her chosen field was very methodical. To be successful you went from point A to point B to point C. But

Matt's world was more haphazard. You could go six months without an audition, then suddenly find yourself with only a few hours to pack before having to get on a plane and report for work. It was an exciting way of life but difficult on relationships. It seemed to Matt that Skylar understood and was the kind of person who could handle the impromptu nature of his business. He sure hoped so because he intended to marry Skylar as soon as she finished her education and he was more financially secure.

So *School Ties* represented one big step toward his future. But for now, Matt just wanted to enjoy the moment. He and Ben went to see the movie in a theater and sat there pinching themselves. There they were, up on the big screen, together. Just the way they had planned it all those years ago. At the time, they couldn't imagine how it could get any better.

# FOUR

While *School Ties* wasn't much of a box office hit, it turned out to be an important career boost for Brendan Fraser, who would continue to find steady work in features. For the other guys, the movie mostly meant money and experience and a chance to develop camaraderie with the other actors.

"It was a group of people who are really fine young actors and who have the same goal: to be the best actors they can be. Plus, they're just a fun bunch of guys."

Matt enjoyed hanging out with his castmates and forged some lasting friendships with many of his co-stars.

"Matt's brilliant and a great guy," says Fraser. "He was the first feature film actor I ever worked with in Hollywood, at the screen test for *School Ties*, and we became friends right away."

But not everyone was interested in hanging out. Damon remembers Chris O'Donnell as being a bit aloof and also very competitive.

"Chris O'Donell was a business major at Boston College and he's a very savvy businessman," Matt says pointedly, then gives an example of what he means.

"The casting for *Scent of a Woman* happened right

during *School Ties*. The whole cast went down to audition for it. The way I found out about the part was, I checked with my agent to see if anything good had come in and he says, 'Well, here's one with a young role and oh my God, it's got Al Pacino in it!' So I go up to Chris and asked if he had heard about the movie.

" 'Yeah.'

" 'Do you have the script?'

" 'Yeah.'

" 'Can I see it?'

" 'No . . . I kind of need it.'

"Chris wouldn't give it to anybody," Damon says, sounding incredulous. "Later, Ben, me, and a bunch of the other guys are commiserating about how our auditions for the movie hadn't gone well. Except for Chris. Chris used to play things very close to the vest. We asked him how his audition went and he just said, 'Oh, it was all right.' He just refused to say how it went."

As they all eventually found out, O'Donnell was cast opposite Pacino and *Scent of a Woman* put Chris on the Hollywood map. The fallout of O'Donnell's good fortune had a demoralizing effect on Matt. Instead of feeling positive about having another movie under his belt, he felt oddly empty.

"Actually, *School Ties* was a bitter pill to swallow because I didn't come out of that a star," he candidly admits. "A lot of people got hot off that movie, but I wasn't one of them. Brendan Fraser and Chris O'Donnell got to be huge out of that movie and I'd be lying if I said there hadn't been some envy there. Yesterday you were hanging out with them and the next day they're these huge movie stars. I thought my performance was pretty good, but I didn't have a publicist, I didn't do many interviews and the phone just didn't ring. It was tough."

Seeing others from what he considered his peer group advance so abruptly made Matt, for the first time, become impatient. And a little broody.

"I wasn't the most gracious person," he acknowledges. "I looked at people all the time and thought, 'Why is that guy working when I'm not?' That's the curse of being a struggling actor. And I'm sure there are actors out there now going, 'What the hell is with this Damon kid? What'd he do? I could do it better.' I totally understand that. There's no parity. Just extreme excesses."

It was the brutality of the profession his parents tried to warn him about. For the most part, Matt accepted the fact that there was a certain element of serendipity and luck involved with acting. But he believed that you could make your own luck if you were prepared enough and good enough.

The upside was that all it took was the one right role, such as what Chris O'Donnell found in *Scent of a Woman*, to send a career skyrocketing. He had been given a small taste of being a film actor and he couldn't wait to get a bigger bite. But waiting for that big break was becoming harder for Matt. He wanted his chance *now* and when it didn't come fast enough, he occasionally became frustrated. Sometimes, it seemed as if the fates were having a laugh at his expense.

"I remember one time during college, they were shooting the movie *With Honors* at Harvard," Damon recalls. Ironically, the movie starred his friend Brendan Fraser, who was yet again playing a student.

"I had auditioned for that movie and almost got it. I was broke and I was so pissed, I couldn't believe I didn't get it. I was like, 'How could you not put me in this movie?'

"And then I wake up one day and just talk about having defeat rubbed in your face, I wake up and they're shooting a scene for the movie right outside my dorm. I walk out to go to my class, I'm late, and somebody says to me, 'Excuse me, don't walk through here.'

"I'm like, 'What?'

"And the person says, 'We're filming a big movie here . . . That you're not in.'

"I was just like going, '*Nooooo!*' inside. It was awful."

Matt kept his mind off of his career frustrations by delving into his school work. In addition to working toward his degree in English, Damon was also active in school drama productions, when his movie schedule permitted.

"Yeah, we did a bunch of plays," Damon says. "I did a Sam Shepard play directed by my professor David Wheeler and I did a play over at the North Theater Company. The last play I did at Harvard was *Burn This*, which was performed in Winthrop House.

"College theater is fun—doing student-directed stuff is great because everybody gets in there together. And I really would have done more and would have liked to do more. I knew people who were doing like two and three shows a semester. I would have done that too, if I would have been guaranteed to stay there the whole semester but a lot of times I wasn't. So they'd say, 'Well, this show is going up in a month,' and if I knew I wasn't leaving in a month, I'd do that show."

Once he got back into the rhythm and routine of college, Damon relaxed and was able to put aside his acting anxieties. It helped that Matt was a naturally gifted student so he was able to easily get back into the academic swing of things.

"Whenever I would go back, I'd usually hit about a 4.0," he admits shyly. "But the grades didn't matter anymore, though. It was just like, '*What a deal!*' Once you get over the idea of how much money you're paying to go to college, it's the most carefree existence.

"I'd take college over going to a spa. It's a lot more interesting. It's basically what I'd do if I were at a spa—read all those books."

Being an English major meant that Matt was also required to do a fair amount of writing assignments. Always anxious to learn as much as he could about anything even remotely acting related, Damon signed up for a playwriting class, even though he did not fancy himself a dramatist.

"I was in a class taught by Anthony Kubiak, who is just an awesome teacher," Matt recalls enthusiastically. "The assignment was to write a one act play as an end-of-the-semester project."

The germ of the idea actually came from his sister-in-law, a graphic artist at MIT, telling him about that school's practice of keeping blackboards in the hall-ways in case a student is suddenly inspired as they walk to a class. That image was Matt's inspiration to create the character Will Hunting, an orphaned roughneck from impoverished South Boston who works as an MIT janitor but is actually a once-in-a-century math genius.

"So I handed this one-act in, which was about forty pages long, and it didn't really go anywhere. But it had a couple of characters in it the teacher liked and he told me I should keep writing it. I kept telling him that I couldn't end it, but he would say that was just because it should be a full-length play and that's how I should write it. So he really encouraged me to continue working on it."

At the time, Matt was taking a theater directing class with David Wheeler. When Ben came back from Los

Angeles, where he was now living, to spend Christmas with his family, Matt showed him the one-act he had written.

"We actually ended up taking it and workshopping it at some acting classes at Harvard with David Wheeler," Damon says. "That's where we first started working it out. Because Ben knows David, he came into the class and we acted it out.

"Then when I was on spring break, in March of 1993, I went to Los Angeles for an audition and while there, showed it to Ben again, and he had the same reaction. He liked it but didn't know where to go with it either," Matt laughs. "But it was then that we made a pact that we would work on it together.

"I had asked a number of people to help, all of them declined, and I was forced to ask Ben," Damon adds, kidding.

"Last guy on the list," Ben says, pretending to have hurt feelings. Then laughs: "I didn't have a job and things weren't looking too good for me so why not?"

"Seriously, though," Damon continues, "Ben, I think, is one of the brightest guys that I know and we have similar sensibilities."

The idea was to work on the play as a kind of long-term project. At the time, Matt was looking at it as more of an intellectual exercise, to see if indeed he and Ben could create a full-length play. Besides, it would be fun to have a project to do with Ben. Not that they needed a reason to stay in touch but it reinforced their bond by having something to work on together.

Even though Ben and Matt had in some respects gone their separate ways after high school, with Matt staying in college in between jobs while Ben chose to ultimately forego higher education and move to Los Angeles, the bond between them had remained intact.

"Matt and I had identical interests, so whether we ended up successful or selling hot dogs at Dodger games, we knew we'd end up doing the same sort of thing," explains Ben. "The remaining friends part was pretty consistent. We saw each other all the time and we talked on the phone all the time."

But having something specific to talk about was special. Suddenly, it felt like they were back in high school in the Media Cafeteria, plotting ways to take Hollywood by storm. They fantasized about writing their own movie that they would get to star in, laughing at the improbability of it. But it was sure fun to dream about.

However, before they could do much more than toss around a few ideas, their work on Matt's play was interrupted when Damon hit what he believed would finally be the career jackpot.

Directed by Walter Hill, with a script by John Milius (*Magnum Force*, *Conan the Barbarian*, and *Apocalypse Now*) and Larry Gross (*48 Hours*) and a cast that included Gene Hackman, Robert Duvall and serious-young-actor-of-the-moment Jason Patric, the feature film *Geronimo* looked like a can't-miss hit. Matt had been selected to play the pivotal role of Second Lt. Britton Davis, a young cavalry officer whose mission is to capture the fierce Apache chief. The movie was based in part on Davis's autobiography.

"It was really awesome to play a character who wrote an autobiography," Damon says. "I must have read the book twenty times."

So while many Damon's classmates prepared to graduate, Matt hit the road to go on location. Even though Damon should have been a member of the Harvard Class of 1992, his acting career meant it would be a while yet before he could graduate.

"What was happening is that I would keep coming back, and I would almost get done with the semester and would be yanked out again," recalls Matt. "So in the spring I left college again to do *Geronimo*. But I thought it was serving me well and everyone at that point was saying the movie was going to be a big hit," Matt says wryly.

It was not only Matt's most important role to date, but it also took him the farthest from home. The movie was shot on location in the desolate beauty of Moab, Utah, the same locations John Ford used for a number of his classic Westerns, including *Cheyenne Autumn* and *Rio Grande*.

When he arrived on location, Matt couldn't quite believe he was going to be working with one of his all time idols, Robert Duvall.

"Working with Duvall was like twenty years of good acting school," Damon says reverentially. "I was taught by him to observe real people, to study from life. He can make things happen without doing much. It comes from his age and experience. I'm still in touch with him. He's a genius."

His experience with another highly regarded actor was less than sublime.

"I only met Gene Hackman once and he called me Mark," Matt laughs.

Like most actors who get to work on Westerns, Matt loved the chance to play cowboys and Indians. But it was a physically strenuous shoot. The production spent three months filming, six days a week. Their wake-up call was five A.M. and most of the actors spent twelve hours riding a horse.

"It was fun," says Damon. "But by the end everybody was ready to get the hell out of there."

As he had done on *Rising Son*, Matt left behind a

solid reputation as a young man willing to work hard and eager to learn. Walter Hill, who teased Damon about being an Ivy Leaguer out on the trails, was impressed with Matt's dedication.

"He was out in the country with the cowboys and Indians and not a lot of those guys had gone to Harvard," Hill jokes. "But he did his work and learned to ride and studied the history of the Apache some. He took the teasing good-naturedly.

"Anyone can truthfully say he's a nice person and a good guy. But what one tends not to see off the bat is what a committed and artistically attuned personality he has."

On paper, there was no reason to think *Geronimo* wouldn't make some serious noise at the box office. *Dances with Wolves* had proven that the Western was still a viable movie genre and Hill had assembled a solid cast and the story of Geronimo, the legendary Apache leader, was full of ready-made drama.

Native Americans lived in what later became known as the American West for hundreds of years before the United States sent soldiers to carry out what was considered America's Manifest Destiny. While many of the tribes were dispossessed of their land without a fight, the Apache leader Geronimo waged what was basically guerrilla warfare against the Army. Geronimo led his thirty-five Chiricahua Apache warriors through southern Arizona chased by 5,000 troops.

Interestingly, the Army was never able to defeat Geromino. He surrendered once, resumed the war, then surrendered a final time. The warrior chief eventually settled in Oklahoma, became a prosperous farmer, and died a natural death at the age of eighty.

But the movie concentrated less on Geronimo himself and more on the daily lives of a band of the Army's professional "Indian fighters." Robert Duvall played a scout named Al Sieber and Jason Patric starred as a young lieutenant named Charles Gatewood with Gene Hackman aboard as Brigadier General George Crook.

The movie follows the Indian fighters' stories for several years as they track and hunt Geronimo's warriors. The film took great pains to refrain from painting Geronimo a murderer by putting the conflict in terms of a war. Yes, the Apache warriors were guilty of killing many white settlers, including women and children, but the U.S. Army had also committed similar atrocities.

Matt's character, Lt. Britton Davis, was the film's narrator. Davis is a young West Point graduate who accompanies Gatewood as they bring Geronimo to an Army settlement; later, after Geronimo resumes his war, they go looking for him again. Eventually, Geronimo, played by Wes Studi, and his few remaining surviving followers are loaded onto a train to be forever taken away from their land.

Despite the film's modernistic take on the life of Geronimo, pitting him as a man defending his homeland and who was repeatedly betrayed by broken promises of the American government, the movie fell flat. Despite being gorgeously filmed, the story wasn't engrossing. *The Washington Post*'s review dissected the film with painful precision.

"Patric's monotone pronouncements are delivered so slowly, softly, and with such sensitivity that you'll come away thinking he's in the Peace Corps, not the cavalry . . .

"The narrative is certainly reverential enough—*it seemed they were chasing a spirit more than a man*. But *Geronimo* is not involving, or heroic; he's a historical cipher who proved as elusive to the filmmakers as he did to the Army . . .

"Cinematographer Ahearn comes up with vistas that are alternately dry dusty browns (for the barren reservations) or look like hand-tinted historical panoramas. But sumptuous backdrops do not a great film make, and neither did Hill. Saddled by Milius and Larry Gross's leaden script and Hill's somnambulant pace, *Geronimo* is hardly better than Ted Turner's recent fiasco," the critic added, referring to a poorly received TNT cable movie about the Apache chief.

*Time* film critic Richard Schickel was kinder but not any more impressed.

"It's the last thing you'd expect to see in the nineties; an old-fashioned cavalry and Indian Western, not so very different from the kind of John Ford and many others used to turn out regularly. All the classic elements are here—harshly beautiful Southwestern landscape, the eponymous warrior chieftain, noble, misused, and off the reservation because promises have been broken; an idealistic young officer, Jason Patric, who respects his enemy; and a greenhorn Matt Damon who wants to learn more about him.

"The script, by Hollywood's last rogue males, John Milius and Larry Gross, devotes too much time to parlay and palaver—to self-justification, if you will. Depending on your point of view, that's either a necessity or a sad commentary on the state of traditional male ways of being."

*Geronimo* was released December 10, 1993 and would be one of the bigger box office disappointments of the year, earning only $13.7 million. Damon's high hopes that this movie would be his career break were quickly deflated as the film only played in theaters a few weeks before sinking to the bottom of the box office charts.

By the time *Geronimo* was collecting dust on the

shelves of video stores, Damon had made the decision to drop out of college and finally pursue his career full-time. But it wasn't an easy decision because Matt was going to miss being in a collegiate atmosphere.

"Let me tell you, I loved Harvard," he says warmly. "It was like a huge, huge part of my life. My time at Harvard was amazing and I still keep in touch with all my college friends."

When asked now if he still plans to finish his degree Damon gives a little laugh and is quick to respond.

"I had to escape to the West Coast to avoid just that question from my mother. I have a year left. I've done it ass-backwards. I'm now getting paid to write, but I would like to go back when I get the chance to get my degree in English, just for the sense of completion. I want to graduate. In an ideal world I'd be too busy to go back but it is something I would like to finish one day."

Then Damon adds, joking, "But if things keep up as they're going, then I should stay working in movies before someone figures out I'm a total charlatan."

In the months after leaving college, Damon would pass his days going on auditions and hanging out with other friends, who were mostly actors. He was also still regularly exchanging ideas with Ben about the play he had started writing in his playwriting class. Although they hadn't really sat down to work on it yet, if nothing else the work in progress at least had a clever name—*Good Will Hunting*—which Matt bought from a friend in Boston who'd suggested it. And despite his intention and determination to develop his play into a full story, for now, Damon was more interested in hunting down the one role that would turn his acting fortunes around.

# FIVE

**After leaving Harvard to go work for three months on** *Geronimo*, Matt never returned to school and officially dropped out of college, just two semesters shy of his degree. Once in Los Angeles, he moved into an apartment with Ben and his younger brother Casey, who was also pursuing an acting career.

Over the next two years, Ben and Matt would live like the stereotypical struggling actors they were, moving from one cheap apartment to another, adding and dropping other roommates, and generally trying to keep each other's spirits up with each passing day that they didn't get an acting job.

Although Los Angeles has a central downtown, business district, the city is made up of a series of neighborhoods that spread from the Pacific Ocean on the West, to the Santa Monica Mountains to the north, to Culver City, the home of the former MGM Studio, on the southern end to the lower income communities of East L.A.

Damon and Ben lived all over, including the Eagle Rock area, which is on the eastern side of the city, a somewhat desolate community probably best known as one of the murderous stomping grounds of the infamous Night Stalker serial killer and maimer. Later, they lived in a small two-bedroom apartment on Curson Avenue, which was more central and near bustling Melrose Avenue, which by then had already adopted its too-hip-for-thou attitude.

But no matter where they lived, they were still struggling actors with very few prospects. Despite their stagnating careers, Ben and Matt were compatible roommates, which is not to say they didn't have their disagreements.

"We lived together in probably ten different apartments at different times in our lives with ten different people who we grew up with and the arguments are always the same," Damon explains. "I'm a slob and I get yelled at for not cleaning up when the house is a mess."

But they were comfortable with each other and most of all, enjoyed facing Hollywood together.

"We've had rises and falls that weren't necessarily meteoric but the word was *us*," Damon explains. "If one of us was working and we had enough money for both of us to go through life, great. The money was there basically to be shared. Ben would be in a series, like eight episodes, he made a little money, great. I did something, I made a little money, great. We were always looking out for each other."

And although money was tight and they would frequently only be able to afford Spam for dinner, Matt says he was never too worried about it.

"There were times when I would worry about the rent, but I never felt I was going to be out on the street," he says. "Our bank accounts would sometimes get down to the point where we needed another job but another job would always come along, although it wasn't always a lot of money."

Matt and Ben's shared background reflected itself in

a number of ways. Besides having similar outlooks about acting and sharing a common work ethic, neither young man was into the trendy, Hollywood club scene, and occasionally, they caught flack for it from some of their more socially-minded friends.

"Ben and I are constantly accused by people who come in and out of our circle, of being the most boring people ever," laughs Damon. "There are people who go, 'I got tickets to go see so-and-so, why don't you guys come?' We're like, 'Yeah, whatever.' They end up at the same bar every night with the same people telling the same jokes. We've always been that way."

Although many struggling actors can become extremely competitive, Matt and Ben never experienced any tension between them, even though they often got called in to read for the same characters. In fact, if Matt were going to lose out on a role to anyone, he would have preferred it be Ben.

"We would go out for the same parts all the time, but it never really came down to a director saying, 'It's either you or Ben,'" Damon says. "It was more like, 'It's Brad Pitt or you.' But in any event you always root for your own guy.

"I hung out with a bunch of actors and I always felt that if I don't get it, I hope someone in the group does, because I thought they were the best guys around and deserved it."

When he wasn't going out on auditions, for the most part, Matt was a bit of a homebody.

"Basically," Casey Affleck says, "Matt sat around, ate Cheerios, played video games, and scribbled in his notebook."

However, Damon wasn't really being as idle as it might have seemed. The notes he was jotting down were ideas for the one-act play he and Ben had put on the back-burner for the past year. But by the spring of 1994, Matt was ready to dust the project off and devote some intense time and energy to it. He was tired and demoralized with how slowly his career was moving.

"If Brad Pitt, Johnny Depp, Leonardo DiCaprio, and every other name guy passed on a script, then maybe I would get to audition," Damon says. "We were living in Eagle Rock. It was a pretty desolate place and we were out there for a couple of years. We were frustrated, because all we got to look at were the scripts everybody on the short list passed on. Then it's you and everyone else brawling for these meager table scraps.

"We finally said, 'Why not just make our own movie? We'll raise the money on our own and it doesn't matter if nobody sees it 'cause when we're feeling bad, we can put this videocassette in and say, 'That's a contribution we made to this field that we love.'"

For as patient as Damon had been with his career during his early years at college, by the beginning of 1994, he was beginning to feel the strain of being stuck in the middle of the pack with the hundreds of other twentysomething young men maneuvering for an acting career. He had expected his career to be further along than it was and with his bank account dwindling and no prospects on the horizon, he knew he needed to take a more active hand in his career.

"The only reason we wrote it was to get jobs. We were living in L.A. and we couldn't get arrested. We were like totally unemployable and we knew it. We couldn't get jobs as actors and felt like we had a lot of energy to put into this career and there was no outlet for it. It was our way of saying, 'Screw the system. We're doing our own thing.'

"That's the frustrating thing about being an actor— you're just not controlling your own destiny. It was like,

'Why are we just sitting here? Let's make our own movie. And if people come to see it, they come, and if they don't, they don't. Either way it beats sitting here going crazy.' "

Ben agrees that it was just the decision to do something, anything constructive that was really a boost to their sagging morale and egos.

"I think more than anything, it was an exercise in frustration," Affleck offers, "because whether or not it actually comes to fruition, I think the act of sitting down and kind of taking control of your own life . . . the problem of being an actor is most of the time you're not going to be working and it's really, really difficult to feel like you own your own life.

"So just the act of sitting down and writing was something we could kind of do on our own time and feel like there was this outlet for this kind of creativity that we felt we had."

Damon had his own personal demons to contend with as well.

"I felt like I had given up college and all these great experiences," he admits. "All my friends had graduated. I had missed out on a lot and here I was back at square one living in L.A. It was really a horrible feeling.

"When you have so much energy and so much passion and no outlet for it and nobody cares, it's just the worst feeling. And there are hundreds and thousands of people like that in Los Angeles, right now. This whole, 'I'm too cool to care' thing you get among young actors in this country is so weak and stupid and played out and it just brings everybody down. You shouldn't be too cool to care, for Christ's sake. You should be full of vim and vigor and trying to do everything you can to make a change."

Obviously, whether he realized it or not, there was a

lot of his mother in Damon. So after letting his unfinished one-act languish unattended for a year, Matt turned his mental energies toward fashioning it into a film vehicle for himself and Ben.

"Yeah, I didn't want to do a movie for myself unless Ben was in it too. So I came up with a character for him that I described as Mercutio," Damons says, referring to Romeo's best friend. "Except in our movie, he wouldn't die. Ben thought that was cool."

Damon says it never crossed his mind to try and write the script on his own without Ben's help.

"No, co-writing was the *only* option because I didn't have the discipline to sit in front of the computer and wait for something to happen. I was an English major in college but that's the extent of my writing background. I didn't write *Good Will Hunting* out of any sense of urgency to write, or any delusion I was good at it. I never made it through college as an English major. I made it through three years.

"I know I can't take a blank page and impose a structure on something. I just can't do it; I'm not put together that way. I know I can't do that because I was an English major. I've written papers for years and I'm just not good at it. It drives me nuts. I pull my hair out in front of the computer watching the cursor blink.

"Writing the script was very easy with him. Ben and I just had this reservoir of common knowledge we could draw on. But I definitely only wrote it out of frustration and desperation—Ben and I simply wanted to create work for ourselves because we couldn't get hired as actors."

Because they were not trained writers, Matt and Ben didn't approach their script in the same way a film school screenwriting graduate would have. Structure and form wasn't their primary concern—simply getting it made so they could finally work in a good project was. Which meant writing it geared to sell.

"We never thought anyone would buy it through Hollywood channels," admits Affleck. "So Matt and I thought that we could really do the movie by raising a little bit of money, like Kevin Smith and Spike Lee and Quentin Tarantino had done."

"Yeah, we sat down and talked about what we needed to do to get the movie made and we knew from what happened with Tarantino's *Reservoir Dogs*, at least what we had read, that it got its money to be made because Harvey Keitel agreed to do it," Damon says.

"So we knew that if we got somebody who was somewhat of a name we could get the movie made. We could at least raise money, even if it wasn't as much as a half-million dollars, even if it was a hundred thousand dollars for a barely known actor. After that, we figured we'd put it together cheaply *à la* Kevin Smith with *Clerks*."

So, in order to attract the attention of a name star who would be attractive to their hoped-for future investors, Matt and Ben wrote a part in their script specifically aimed at the biggest target.

"To help sell it, we wrote the part of a psychiatrist for a thirty- to fifty-year-old man because that's the demo of Hollywood's biggest, most established stars," explains Affleck. "We were thinking we'd get it to these top stars, they'd read the script, love it and help it get made for us. We were thinking naively," he adds.

But the point was, they were thinking, and finally doing something that made them feel more in control and less at the mercy of others. For them, writing wasn't a solitary exercise but an extended acting exercise. They largely developed the script by acting out the various roles in their living room.

"We didn't have a formula," Matt admits. "Because we roomed together, we didn't really have any hard, fast writing schedule. We never forced ourselves to write. We would just sit down haphazardly, and a lot of times we wouldn't even be at a computer. Sometimes we'd just be sitting there and strike up a conversation over lunch and we'd come up with a scene that way. Then we'd go home and write it down. There was absolutely no rhyme or reason to it.

"There were a lot of times when Ben and I just improv'd. We'd take a tape recorder, put it down, and just start improvising. We'd stand up and act out whatever scene we were working on. There was a lot of throwing stuff against the wall and seeing what stuck. We really go moment to moment as actors and that's what made the process interesting for me. It came down to, what would be fun to act?

"Eventually, we might come up with a half-hour improv out of which we might have fifteen seconds that were good. We'd be looking through the tape and suddenly go, 'Yeah, yeah, yeah! That's it. That one. Write it down.' And maybe a scene would start from that line."

Affleck has admitted that on occasion, they were just as busy partying as they were writing.

"Mostly, we'd just get drunk," he laughed. "And as the night went on, the writing got better and better. Then the next day, we're like, 'Hey, I don't remember this scene but it's really good!' "

For the most part, Affleck was responsible for the manual labor of putting their work into script form.

"Ben's a faster typist than I am, so a lot of times what would end up happening was he'd sit in the chair for the actual typing segment, but we pretty much would both sit by the computer."

Once they were into reworking the one-act into a

movie script, their *Good Will Hunting* project became a priority. Even so, it was a slow process.

"Altogether, I bet we have got a thousand pages of Will Hunting on the computer," Damon laughs. "We have Will going to the zoo, we have Will being chased by government agents, we even have Will being killed. Ben and I just tried to see what would work—and most of it didn't."

The original script for *Good Will Hunting* was actually a political thriller.

"Yeah, absolutely. We basically superimposed this kind of ridiculous structure on it just because we were trying to get it made."

In his early incarnation, Will was a mathematical genius who attracts the unwanted interest of evil government agents.

"When we originally wrote it, we thought in order for us to get it made we would have to Hollywood it up," explains Ben. "So we had two FBI-type surveillance teams following him and we had the National Security Agency interested in his gift for their nefarious schemes. There was also more comedy. It was a different kind of movie than it would later become."

However, despite the thriller aspect of their original script, they weren't really writing an action movie.

"No, because what interests us, as actors, is the moment-to-moment honesty in scenes," says Damon. "That's basically why *I* go to movies. I mean, I'm not a snob," he quickly points out. "I like to see an explosion chase every once in a while too. And there are a lot of writers who do that very well. But in terms of what we were working on, we kind of stuck with simple scenes and with what we knew."

So they set the action in an environment both Ben and Matt were intimately familiar with—Boston, the world of academia, and the rougher edges of the life among the city's blue-collar neighborhoods. By doing that, they were able to communicate in a kind of emotional shorthand, which helped move the writing along.

While collaborating on the script, Matt and Ben continued to make their rounds of auditions and occasionally get work. But even work didn't deter them from working on the script.

"At one point, I ran out of money and I took a job that ended up being a wonderful job," recalls Damon. "It was a TNT movie called *The Good Old Boys* that Tommy Lee Jones directed. The only bad part was I was stuck in Alpine, Texas."

But thanks to modern technology, Matt and Ben were able to keep plugging away at their script, pinning their hopes on what they believed would be their chance to finally make a name for themselves and stand out from the rest of the crowded pack.

# SIX

**Alpine, Texas, is truly located in the middle of nowhere,**
which is partly its claim to fame and appeal. Situated at
the edge of the great Chihuahuan Desert in the high
desert country of West Texas, the town is the northern
gateway to Big Bend Country and the renowned Big
Bend National Park. Originally named Murphysville in
1883, the town was renamed in 1888 to reflect its location in what local settlers called the "Alps of Texas."

Alpine's natural scenic wonders, which include
rugged mountains and Rio Grande canyons, has made
the area a popular filming location for decades. In
1955, the movie *Giant*, starring Rock Hudson, James
Dean, and Elizabeth Taylor was filmed in nearby Marfa,
a half-hour drive away.

But with only 6,200 full-time residents, Alpine is still
a small town, despite the presence of a golf course and
local university, Sul Ross State University, which is
proud to be the birthplace of the National Intercolle-
giate Rodeo Association.

For Matt, it was just another out-of-the-way location.
Even so, he still managed to find a way to work with
Ben on their script.

"There was one fax machine in the entire town run
by this Iranian guy named Rajou," he recalls. "I used to

go to him and he would send my fax away for me. He drove a Lexus and it was the only Lexus in West Texas. And his license plate read RAJOU. Anyway, Rajou was our middleman for our scripts for a few months."

Instead of acting out the prospective scenes together in their living room, Matt and Ben were forced to put their ideas down in writing.

"Ben would fax me scenes, which I'd look at and then make notes. It would give me ideas and I'd send that back to Ben. Then we'd call each other on the phone and talk about what worked and what didn't. 'All right, now I see from this scene we need this other scene . . . Okay, I'll work on that. Tomorrow they're shooting a scene I'm not in so I'll have a couple of hours to do that and I'll fax it to you at the end of the day.' That's how it went."

In between working on the screenplay, Matt had a movie to shoot. When he had first been hired on the film, Matt felt as if he's actually taken a step backward in his career.

"I've had to eat crow a few times and this was one of them," he says with an edge. "When I went back to TNT for this movie, I was making less money than I made when I was nineteen on *Rising Son*.

"But I couldn't say '*I won't do it*' because I was broke. It paid me $20,000 and that was more than I could make that summer painting houses. Meanwhile, I was watching my contemporaries make a boatload of money doing whatever they wanted. It was really hard."

As it turned out, *The Good Old Boys* was a wonderful experience for Matt. For one thing, he was surrounded by a cast of quality actors, including future Oscar-winner, Frances McDormand, Sam Shepard, former Oscar-winner Sissy Spacek, who had starred with Jones in *Coal Miner's Daughter*, and Wilford Brimley.

The film was Tommy Lee Jones's, directorial debut—he also co-wrote the teleplay and starred as the lead character, Hewey Calloway—and he had surrounded himself with a cast of actors he knew personally and who he knew would make him look good. Set in turn-of-the-century Texas and based on a novel by Elmer Kelton, the story revolves around Hewey, a twentieth-century cowboy who fought alongside Teddy Roosevelt in Cuba.

After being away for two years, Hewey shows up on his brother Walter's financially troubled farm and gets a cool greeting, especially from Walter's unhappy wife, Eve, played by Frances McDormand. While staying with his brother, Hewey finds himself attracted to the new schoolteacher in town, Spring Renfro (Sissy Spacek), and most of the movie focuses on their relationship. Damon was aboard as Hewey's nephew, Cotton Calloway, who leaves his family behind to pursue his passion for automobiles.

A small film even by cable standards, it was also very well critically received. *Entertainment Weekly's* TV critic, Ken Tucker, praised the attention to details.

"This is the rare sort of modern movie that turns a scene of neighbors sitting around chatting while eating homemade ice cream into a lovely moment you wish wouldn't end. It's a sweet-tempered film, but it isn't drippy; when a woman snaps, 'Kinda cowboys we got around these days, a woman'd be better off with a good dog and a hot-water bottle,' you know she's not kidding around.

"*Boys* has its action scenes—a fistfight or two, a pretty exciting steer-roping competition—but it works best as a set of character studies. Its small-scale virtues are so quirky and novel as to constitute a constant, happy surprise."

Janis D. Froelich of the Gannett News Service was even more vocal in her praise. "*The Good Old Boys* is a fine cable movie that could well have played in movie houses. It's that good. Jones' performance is so wonderful a viewer loses sight of the fact that this is indeed the same Jones who blew away audiences with his powerful detective in *The Fugitive* . . . This is TV worth making popcorn for."

As he had a knack for doing, Matt managed to impress his coworkers with his desire to learn and his abilities. Alan Caso, the film's cinematographer, recalls Damon as an ambitious go-getter.

"With Matt Damon, you could tell right off the bat that this kid had things going for him. He's a smart kid and really focused. I thought then, for sure, this guy is a talent for the future."

But Matt was getting tired of waiting for his future to arrive. Although he enjoyed working on *The Good Old Boys*, the aftermath was yet another exercise in frustration. While the movie was generating praise and attention, with Tommy Lee Jones and Sissy Spacek justifiably being singled out by reviewers, once again Matt came away with little to show for his efforts. He felt a little like an invisible man.

It's not that he cared about the size of the role so much, but that the roles he was getting didn't stand out. That frustration is what prompted him to actually turn down work in what many thought would be a successful feature, Sharon Stone's *The Quick and the Dead*.

Matt was actually offered the role, which for most struggling actors would have been considered a major coup. But Damon didn't like the script and chose to pass. His agents were understandably shocked and Matt remembers trying to explain his reasoning to them.

"You know what I did last night?" he told them. "I

watched *Bullitt*. Robert Duvall drives a cab in that movie and he has like four lines, but he was totally believable and he was really good and at the end of the day, he was in *Bullitt*. He is in all these great movies because he doesn't do *this* kind of thing." "This" being *The Quick and the Dead*.

And as it turned out, Damon's instinct about the script turned out to be dead-on. The film was greeted with a tepid response from moviegoers and was quickly making its way to video store shelves. And the role he turned down? Ironically, the part eventually went to Leonardo DiCaprio. For once, someone else had picked up Matt's leftovers.

Once back home, Matt and Ben put even more energy into the script. Not only were they out-of-work actors, they were also single, unattached guys again.

"I was a total failure with the girls," Affleck admits, although he was briefly engaged in the early 1990s. "It was a catastrophe. Matt was the one with all the girls calling."

That's because Damon's longtime relationship with Skylar had ended when she broke off their engagement. Although Matt was heartbroken, in his heart he had to know that it would be next to impossible to maintain the relationship with her living in New York and him struggling to put food on the table in Los Angeles.

When he had dropped out of Harvard and moved West, it had put a huge strain on their relationship.

"It was a long-distance romance, which was really hard, although we had already been doing it for years."

But Cambridge, Massachusetts, is a lot closer to Manhattan than Los Angeles is and it was only a matter of time before he and Skylar began drifting apart. However, when Skylar made the Dear John phonecall, it still came as a shock to Matt to hear his fiancée had met someone else and fallen in love. What made the news even more ego-deflating was that the new man in her life was not only successful, but rich. Lars Ulrich was the drummer for the mega-popular heavy metal band, Metallica. Skylar and Lars would eventually get married in Las Vegas in February 1997.

"Yeah, she married a rock star . . . who's got $80 million and his own jet," Damon says with uncharacteristic bitterness. Then he added, "She was the love of my life," he said of Skylar, who is now a doctor of internal medicine and still married to Ulrich.

By the autumn of 1994, Matt and Ben finally had a finished script. It hadn't been easy. For one thing, they had encountered a surprising amount of resistance to their plan.

"I think a lot of people start out trying to write their own way," Ben suggested. "People told us we were making a mistake, that it would never work out, that it went against conventional wisdom. We just went ahead anyway.

"Stallone set the precedent for us. It's kind of difficult to go to Hollywood with a script and you're not really impressing a lot of people when you walk in and say, 'This is mine, man.' They look at you like, 'What, are you retarded? There's no way you're going to be in it.' They want to put all these other stars in it."

And there had been times when it seemed as if they would never have a cohesive script and they became disheartened at how hard it was to put the script together.

"We definitely had to pick each other up at certain points," Matt acknowledges. "Though it seemed like just when one of us was about to give up, that's when the other one was getting his second wind."

By the time they had a screenplay that was ready for

others to see, their financial situation was looking particularly bleak. Even though Matt had recently signed on for a small part in an upcoming movie starring Denzel Washington and Meg Ryan, the pay would be minimal.

"We were absolutely flat broke and we were looking for cash. I mean, it couldn't have gotten any worse. We were planning to break the lease on the house where we were living because this place was a little expensive for us," admits Damon. "And in relative terms, it wasn't a very expensive house. We had a tiny little place in West Hollywood and here's Ben at six-foot-four sleeping on my couch and not fitting in it. It was a pathetic sight."

One of the first people to see the first version of *Good Will Hunting* was agent-turned-producer Chris Moore, who Ben met while starring as the lead in the independent feature, *Glory Daze*. Matt also appeared in the film, playing the unfortunately named Edgar Pudwhacker. As the character's name indicates, *Glory Daze* was a *National Lampoon*-esque movie about a bunch of college buddies who would prefer to stay adolescents as long as they can rather than join the real world as adults.

And right off the bat, Matt and Ben's script got the response they'd been hoping for.

"I was making *Glory Daze* soon after we finished the screenplay and I showed it to Chris and he committed to make it for $1 million if we couldn't get more money elsewhere."

Emboldened by that good news, Matt decided to ask his agent to read the script. "I think we weren't the first actors to tell their agent, 'We wrote a script.' We were thinking he was like, 'Oh, you don't say . . . you have a script. Wonderful.' But he read it out of a feeling of total obligation, and probably dread."

"And then he decided, 'Well, you know, it's not any worse than any of the other scripts,' " adds Ben. "And so he just decided to try and sell it.

"Yeah, he really liked it," Matt says, picking up the story. "So my agent gave it to the literary department and they started the bidding war."

On November 13, 1994, the *Good Will Hunting* script became the object of an intense bidding war in Hollywood.

"When the phone started ringing, we were ready to take the first offer, which was $15,000," says Affleck.

"And after each call, we were yelling at our agent, Patrick Whitesell, *'Take it. Just take the offer!'* " recalls Damon. "As it turned out, we were offered a lot of money to bow out but obviously, that wasn't something we were interested in doing. The only thing that mattered to Ben and me was that we were in it."

Part of the reason they could hold out in the face of vast sums of money being offered to them if they would only give up their dream to act in the film, was that in their hearts, they believed they had a safety net.

"You have a lot of power if you don't need the Industry," Matt says. "Ben had done a movie, *Glory Days*, which literally made $723. It got made by selling $20,000 units to doctors and lawyers. They made the film for $800,000. And the investors at least made their initial investment back on video and foreign sales. So we knew we could get *Good Will Hunting* made that way because we had the same connections through Chris Moore.

"It was a given we would star in our own movie. We didn't need the studios. That's empowerment. For once, we weren't begging for a job."

For four days, Matt and Ben watched in amazement as various studios made them offers.

"This whole bidding war erupted out of nowhere. One day Ben and I were on the couch sharing a chicken sandwich and four days later we sold the script for an incredible amount of money. Thank God for agents. The first day they were offering us like twenty bucks and a pack of cigarettes and Ben and I were like, '*Take it, man!*'

"But the agent went off and said, 'No, that's too low for these guys. They want a *lot* higher.' Then it went sky high," says Damon, still sounding amazed. "Thank God for these agents because we really would have taken anything that was offered. We would have taken a piece of chicken. So they stopped telling us what was happening until the very end.

Fortunately for them, during those four days, Ben and Matt didn't have to just sit around and wait.

"We were going to the studios that were interested, and we took all these meetings because what they really wanted to know [was how serious we were about] saying we're going to be in it. [That was] our only criterion.

"And so they'd say, 'Well, we want to meet you then.' So we'd go to these meetings and talk about the script and they'd either say, 'Yeah, we'll buy this movie and let you be in it' or some studios exercised their right not to buy a movie with two unknown guys in it and that's cool too. We understand the business aspect.

"It was the first time we realized how Hollywood really works. We'd both gone in for a lot of auditions, but when you actually have something people are trying to buy from you, it's a whole different thing."

Damon says the names mentioned most by the studios as who they envisioned in the role of Will Hunting were Brad Pitt and Leonardo DiCaprio.

"*Courage Under Fire* hadn't come out yet. I was actually just starting to lose weight for it. People knew enough to be like, 'Yeah, people have employed these guys before,' but Ben's last movie was *Mallrats* and mine was *The Good Old Boys* for TNT. People certainly weren't like, 'Let's get these two knuckleheads to headline our movie.' And they certainly weren't going to pay a lot of money for it and then give away the best two parts to us," Damon explains.

Affleck adds: "The really sort of outrageous thing was that nobody knew who we were," Ben says. "They said, 'This is great; we think we could get some really good actors for this.' And we're going, 'No, no, no—we're the actors.' And they were like, 'Oh, you're the actors? That's sweet. That's cute.' "

An offer of one million dollars was put on the table, but only if Damon and Affleck agreed to just sell the screenplay outright, there was not a moment of hesitation before they said no.

"We never once thought about taking the money and running," claims Matt. "We thought a lot about Sylvester Stallone. There's a famous story about him before *Rocky* got made. He had $103 in the bank and a pregnant wife and they offered him $30,000 for the *Rocky* script if he walked away. They wanted the movie for Ryan O'Neal. Stallone said no and stuck to his guns. Every time they'd say *A million dollars*, we'd say, *Rocky!*"

Which is not to say turning down money didn't cause them extreme anxiety.

"Sure, we were afraid on a human level it was going to fall apart," admits Damon. "We were talking about the difference between eating Spam and being able to buy a three-bedroom house with a pool table and new car."

But finally, a deal was worked out and by Friday, Matt and Ben had agreed to accept the offer given by Castle Rock Entertainment.

"A lot of people were advising us that Castle Rock was the place to go at the time and so that's what we did," Matt explains. "We went with the place that we thought was the smartest place for our movie.

"It was such a big thing, our agent actually came to the house. He came to finish up the deal on the phone. Then there was this moment when the phone rang and we thought it was Castle Rock and Patrick picked it up and it was for my roommate . . . it was this girl he had dated in college and we were like, 'Hang up the f---ing phone!' He was really bummed because they hadn't talked in three years," Damon says, laughing at the memory.

Matt and Ben were paid $600,000 for *Good Will Hunting*, which meant that after the agents' commissions, they were each approximately $250,000 richer.

"We got more money than we'd ever had," Matt says, then adds pointedly. "And yet, they paid us a lot less than they would have if we'd not been in it."

Even though they knew the deal was firm, both Matt and Ben had a hard time grasping all that had just happened to them. But one thing for sure, they knew it was time to celebrate.

"Oh, man, when we finally sold the script we had everybody over to our house," laughs Damon. "It was warm Pabst Blue Ribbon beer for everybody."

One of the first to congratulate Matt was Chris Moore, who the boys had attached to the project as their producer.

"Chris brought over a bottle of champagne that he had had for three years, a bottle he had been given when he left agenting and was told not to open until his new life as a producer had started."

Matt admits it took a while for the full impact of the money to sink in. "They had given us so much [frigging] money, we didn't even know what to do. One of my actor friends came over and read about us on the front page of *Variety* and he goes, 'We're going to Sizzler.' That was it. We just got in the car and went to Sizzler for an all-you-can-eat shrimp dinner for about $6.99.

"I mean, we sold the script for a little over a half million and we go from eating Ramen Pride to eating real spaghetti. It was amazing. But the first thing we did when we got the money was get out of that house. We moved into another house that had four bedrooms. We had two other roommates and they were there the year we leased the house—and didn't pay a nickel of rent. One was an actor, who has since quit to go into the world of sports broadcasting."

Even though they would soon have bulging bank accounts, Matt and Ben were still their old non-Hollywood, non-slick selves. Their manner was so laid-back that they caught a few of the Castle Rock executives by surprise.

"When we first walked in for our first meeting, the executives took one look at us and said, 'Do you guys want an advance?'" Damon laughs.

Aside from the money and the peace of mind and freedom it gave Matt and Ben, what was really important about selling *Good Will Hunting* was that for the first time since he had moved to Los Angeles, Matt felt in control of his life as an actor. The irony didn't escape him that to do that, he had to turn to writing.

"An actor's existence, unlike a writer's, can be really debilitating in the sense that you don't control when you work. A writer can sit down and write any time they want to, and an actor really can't do that. I mean, you *can* perform monologues in your own living room for your cat, but it's not really the same thing.

"Writing was, for us, a really good thing, just to

maintain our sanity. It will stay that. And making no kind of grand proclamations about what we might write, it really informs us as actors too. I'm a better actor because I did this. On a set I can talk to a writer in a whole new way, I think and have a whole new respect for what they do.

"And after five years of getting pummeled like George Foreman in the ring with Muhammad Ali, it was great to feel like I finally won a round."

# SEVEN

**Despite achieving minor celebrity status as one of the** unknowns who sold Castle Rock the *Hunting* script in 1994, Matt was still struggling to break out as an actor. Although the script had been sold, now came the long process of reworking it to Castle Rock's satisfaction via rewrites.

But first, Matt had a part to prepare for. Shortly before the bidding had started on *Good Will Hunting*, Damon had been cast in a small role for the film *Courage Under Fire*. The film, to be directed by Edward Zwick (*Glory, Legends of the Fall*) and written by Patrick Sheane Duncan (*Mr. Holland's Opus*), was the first Hollywood theatrical release to be set in the Gulf War, or Operation Desert Storm.

Once again, he would be working alongside quality talent, in this case Denzel Washington, Lou Diamond Phillips, and Meg Ryan. But unlike any of the other roles he had played, this one required him to change his look—drastically. Because in the film, he was to portray a young soldier who becomes a heroin addict

"It was a before and after thing," explains Damon. "Some of the shots were supposed to be from Desert Storm and then the other shots were to show what happened to this guy afterwards. I wanted to make it a marked difference between what essentially was two different characters. So I decided to play one guy at 180 pounds and the other at 139 pounds. Ed Zwick, the director, really wanted to cut from my face as one to my face as the other to show the ravaging effects of the guy's heroin addiction."

Damon had three months to lose the weight but instead of doing it under a doctor's supervision, he silently chose to go it alone.

"What happened was at the time I wasn't really a big enough actor for the studio to pay for a nutritionist," Matt surmised. "And I didn't have the money to pay for one. So I just decided to do it myself. I was twenty-five and was like, 'I'll just do it. I'll be all right.' Now, I would get a nutritionist. In fact, I don't really want a nutritionist now and they give me one anyway."

Even though he can joke about it now, it was a risky undertaking. But as far as Matt was concerned, it was something he felt he had to do.

"It was a business decision. I thought, nobody will take this role because it's too small. So if I go out of my way to make something of this role . . .

"It was that thing I think a lot of actors have; this gnawing feeling of self-worth but no place to express it. So even though it was a very small job on paper, I was willing to kill myself just because I wanted to be heard of."

Damon believed that if he made the role of the medic, Ilario, striking enough, maybe someone would finally take notice of him as an actor. He didn't believe it should be necessary to land a starring role in order to earn a reputation as a quality actor.

"Benicio Del Toro is killed early in the movie *The Usual Suspects* and he has maybe nine lines," Matt points out. "But I found it the most memorable performance of 1995. The guy just goes out and thinks, 'Nobody is going to understand what I'm doing except me, but I'm a f---ing genius.' "

Damon decided on a two-prong regimen in order to lose the weight—severely restricting his daily caloric intake and burning extra calories through strenuous exercise.

"It was the most discipline of anything that I've ever done in my life, by far. For three months, I ate nothing but egg whites, chicken, vegetables, and one dry baked potato a day. I'd run six miles in the morning and another six in the afternoon. It was really dangerous because I was fainting every time I stood up." But he says he had no choice but to make his diet so rigorous and austere.

"It evolved essentially because there was a light at the end of the tunnel. There was a time limit because the movie was going to begin production at a specified date.

"Given that, the person who outlined the diet for me didn't think I'd be able to stick to it. It was too difficult. And then when I stuck to it, people got worried. 'You have to eat. You have to be fit. You really have to be prepared.' And I refused to do so. 'Why eat? I've come this far, I'm not going to stop now.'

On Thanksgiving Day in 1994, Matt celebrated by going for a thirteen mile run. Not only were his friends concerned Matt was overdoing it, but so was his family.

"He was obsessive about it," says his brother Kyle. "I'm genuinely worried about him because I know he will sacrifice himself for other characters."

His mother had other concerns besides Matt's decision to lose weight for the role, such as how the film would present the Desert Storm conflict.

"It was hard for me to go to the set of *Courage Under Fire*," says Carlsson-Paige. "I was deeply against the

Gulf War and I didn't know how the film was going to pan out politically."

By the time Matt reported for work, he had so altered his appearance he genuinely looked like a junkie, or as if he was suffering from a life-threatening illness. Matt had lost forty pounds for what would be a scene that would only take two days to film.

"I was under two percent body fat," Damon reveals. "I remember seeing Lou Diamond Phillips (who boxed in the film) and thinking, God, if I looked like that I wouldn't take my shirt off. I thought he looked fat!"

Matt's commitment to the role and the physical sacrifices he was making for it did not go unnoticed.

"It was amazing to watch his discipline," says Lou Diamond Phillips. "He kept to a diet of steamed chicken breast and steamed vegetables and that's it. Matt likes to eat so this was a huge undertaking for him."

But it was the kind of movie that Matt instinctively knew was going to garner a lot of attention and he was determined to make whatever screen time he had noteworthy.

In the film, Denzel Washington plays Lieutenant Colonel Nathaniel Serling, a tank commander in the Gulf War who mistakenly ordered friendly fire on his own men during the confusion of battle at a spot called Al Bathra. His fatal error results in the death of Serling's closest friend.

The lieutenant is further shaken when he realizes the military is trying to cover up the incident when he is transferred to a desk job in Washington and ordered not to speak publicly about the incident while it is allegedly under investigation.

While dealing with his own guilt and conscience, Serling is given the task of investigating possible candidates for the Medal of Honor, in particular, whether the death in battle of medevac helicopter pilot Captain Karen Walden, played by Meg Ryan, warrants the nation's highest military honor. Serling finds himself under intense political pressure because many high-ranking officials in the government believe it would be politically expedient to have Walden become the first woman to get this preeminent combat decoration.

Initially, the investigation appears to be routine, but the more Serling investigates, the more inconsistencies he uncovers. It's at this point the movie uses a dramatic convention made famous in Akira Kurosawa's 1950 classic film, *Rashomon*, in which *Courage Under Fire* tells and retells the story of the incident, in which Walden dies in the Iraqi desert while trying to rescue stranded U.S. troops, from different character's viewpoints.

Eventually, the truth is revealed, in part by Damon's character, who has become a heroin addict because of the guilty knowledge he has about Walden's death, which concerns Monfriez, a gung-ho noncommissioned officer, played by Lou Diamond Philips, whose mistrust of women in battle leads him to challenge Walden and treat her with ever-escalating hostility and violence. While on the rescue mission, Monfriez snaps and shoots Walden in a fit of rage. The other men in her crew, frightened for themselves, agree to leave her behind to die. In the end, as Serling prepares to arrest Monfriez, the officer kills himself by driving his speeding car head-first into an oncoming train.

Although Damon's role was small, it was pivotal to the story. And it was played opposite Washington. So despite being extremely weak, Damon was still excited to have the opportunity to work with the Oscar-winning actor. He was also very nervous.

"I was very intimidated working with Denzel. I almost couldn't talk. I have a habit of quoting lines to people from their movies and that's what I did to Denzel. In these scenes I was sitting across from Denzel. And I started doing a speech from *Malcolm X*—'We didn't land on Plymouth Rock, Plymouth Rock landed on us.' And he started doing it back to me. So that was really a big kick for me. He loosened me up really fast that way."

But Matt's health was so precarious, he literally fainted every time he stood up. Known as a bit of a joker when not working, Denzel played it straight with Matt, whose condition was obviously weakened by the severe weight loss.

"Denzel was telling me that when Tom Hanks lost all that weight to play a character with AIDS in *Philadelphia*, he filled his briefcase with Milky Ways and opened it off-camera while Hanks was on the stand in the courtroom scene, looking like he was about to die. But Denzel knew he couldn't do that to me."

The scene shot with Washington was filmed over the course of two days and is haunting in its power. And once it was over, Matt thought it would be okay to immediately start eating as much as he wanted.

"At the end of the movie, I started eating chocolate cake. Literally, the day after I shot the scene with Denzel Washington walking on the lake, I started eating four or five chocolate cakes, twelve beers, four steaks, tons of pasta. I would eat a chocolate cake and wash it down with a steak. And my stomach expanded.

"I should have put the weight back on gradually, but I couldn't. Once I turned the discipline switch off, that was it."

Besides, Damon knew he had only three weeks to regain most of the weight he had lost before Zwick would be shooting the Gulf War scenes, which would depict Ilario at a normal, pre-junkie weight. It would take almost a month to film the combat scenes.

"There were days when I thought, Oh, God, is this ever going to end? Because it would take so long to set up the action shots."

Ironically, it was his ravenous hunger even more so than the drastic weight loss, that put Damon in harm's way.

"That's how I got sick, by eating again," Damon explains. "It was really stupid. When the doctor finally sat me down after it, he said, 'Well the good news is that your heart didn't shrink.' Then he ran all these tests."

The doctor informed Matt that he had caused serious, but fortunately not permanent damage to himself.

"I overtaxed my adrenal system. I'd be sleeping and get flashes of heat and then a charge of adrenaline. My body thought the bear was chasing it. I had to go on medication for dizziness, lightheadedness, stress, post-traumatic stress disorder. And I was on the medication for a full two years. That taught me a lot about what I can and can't do, what I should and shouldn't do."

Damon had put himself on the line for the role and once back home, waited for the film to come out. And as expected, the movie opened to mostly critical praise, with some reviewers taking note of Damon's performance.

"*Courage Under Fire* is a great film, a powerful film, a haunting excursion that grabs you by the lapels and holds on tight," exclaimed Mike Pearson of the *Rocky Mountain News*.

"Washington is first-rate, skillfully fleshing out a role that's truly colorblind. Ryan has less screen time, but her scenes are marked by a festering tension. The supporting cast makes *Courage* even more compelling: Lou Diamond Phillips as a malevolent gunner with something to hide; Michael Moriarty as Nat's between-a-rock-and-a-hard-place superior; Matt Damon as the junkie medic who knows too much."

Roger Ebert singled Matt out for words of praise. "Matt Damon is also engrossing as Ilario, whose nervous admiration of Walden hides its own secrets."

But in many of the reviews, especially the more important papers such as the *Los Angeles Times*, Matt's name isn't even mentioned.

"Intelligent, involving, and serious, it is as honestly emotional as Hollywood allows itself to get, a story of the search for wartime truth whose own concern for the genuine makes all the difference," enthused Kenneth Turan, the *Times'* film critic..

"*Courage* also benefits from the strength of its supporting players. Lou Diamond Phillips gives an intense, focused performance as Monfriez, a crew member with an essential piece of information, and Scott Glenn adds believability to the standard sequences of a probing *Washington Post* reporter. Just as impressive is Michael Moriarty, rarely seen in features these days, who gives a convincing spin to the often pro forma role of the powerful commanding officer, General Hershberg."

"After *Courage Under Fire* came out, a lot of buzz went around the movie," Matt says. "Denzel Washington, Meg Ryan, and Lou Diamond Phillips all got a lot of attention. I didn't have a publicist back then. It was Denzel Washington who would go out and publicly say, 'This kid . . .' and he would mention me. I thought, That's it. My phone didn't ring for six months."

To be so thoroughly overlooked, particularly in light of the fact that he had literally put his life on the line for the role, was almost more than Matt could bear.

"I wanted to quit acting after that," he says, seriously. "I was really demoralized."

But what kept Damon from throwing in the towel was the knowledge that he had *Good Will Hunting* waiting in the wings. So after the initial disappointment wore off, he was able to appreciate the experience afforded him by *Courage Under Fire*.

"With Denzel, I learned a ton. I only worked with him for two days. But it was amazing the amount of information that got passed to me being in a scene with him. That is when you really learn. You can really get into the minutiae of what is going on."

And as usual, Damon impressed people with his commitment and talent.

"On his first day of shooting, after his first scene with Denzel, Denzel and I looked at each other and we both knew what was registering with us—*this is the real deal*," says Ed Zwick, who knows a little something about discovering talent. Zwick was responsible for the ground-breaking television series, *thirtysomething* which helped launch the careers of Ken Olin, Peter Horton, Mel Harris, and Patricia Wettig.

Zwick adds, "There have been moments, when you meet someone for the first time and their talent is immediate. When Matt walked in, it was so abundantly clear that he had the abilities."

In retrospect, Damon knows that in many ways, it was foolhardy to lose so much weight without medical supervision and he appreciates the fact that his health could have been permanently impaired had he not been so healthy to begin with. But on the other hand, it was something he needed to do for himself.

"I liked the role and so I worked for the role. It cost a lot to get there but for me, it was worth it. I was sick of reading scripts that Chris O'Donnell had passed on and I was looking for something to set me apart. 'Look at what I'll do. I'll kill myself.' And directors took note of that.

"I'm glad that I stuck with it and I don't regret it," he says, then adds, "But I'd never do it like that again."

# EIGHT

**After the initial euphoria of having sold the *Good Will Hunting***
script dissipated, Matt and Ben were left facing the real
hard part of moving making—developing the script to
the studio's liking. What they couldn't possibly know was
that writing and selling of *Hunting* had actually been the
easy part of the process.

"I never understood how movies could take that long
to get made," Damon admits. "I would hear stories
about development hell and think, That's not me."

And, indeed, their initial impression of Castle Rock
was very favorable. Castle Rock founding partner Rob
Reiner and Liz Glotzer, president of production at the
company, told them to lose the thriller element. Reiner
advised Matt in particular to concentrate on the relationship between Will and his psychiatrist.

"Rob and Liz told us to lose the thriller element, to
make the movie smaller and more personal," Matt
recalls, "They said, 'It's okay to make this story very
small.' And we were really lucky that we went to him
first because I don't think anybody else would have suggested that. There were other studios who were much
more interested in making it *more* of a thriller."

It wasn't as if either Ben or Matt had been emotion-
ally tied to the thriller aspect of the script in the first

place. They had incorporated it strictly out of presumed expediency.

"We had inserted that element to help sell the script," Ben points out. "We were lucky enough to run into people who were smart enough to say, 'You don't need that. Stick to writing real people and don't trick it up with all this other stuff.' Even though we were reluctant at first because we thought action was what everyone was supposed to want. We figured we needed an antagonist. We didn't know that you were allowed to make a movie without a bad guy. We didn't think anyone would do that."

Having to work to others' specification was an exercise in discipline for Matt and Ben. But unlike many professional screenwriters who become possessive and defensive of their work, Damon and Affleck exhibited very little personal ego—they simply wanted to make the best film possible.

"It was really an interesting experience," Matt says of the development process. "We approached it as, 'This really isn't our forte, we'd rather just hear what you have to say about it.' And we listened to people's opinions. A lot of it was listening to notes and *not* making changes too.

"Then it was a matter of personal taste. I mean, we did get into a fair amount of brawls in those rooms defending certain things. Sometimes defending the wrong things and then stepping away for a little while and saying, 'Oh, I see what they're saying.' "

Because of their inexperience, the executives at Castle Rock were anxious for Matt and Ben to have some seasoned guiding hands. For Damon especially, it was a thrill to meet writers and moviemakers whose films he had long admired.

"There were a lot of really good meetings. We met a

lot of really good writers," Damon enthuses. "There were a lot of people who were friends of the court who came in and threw in their two cents for us, which was great. It was really helpful."

Among the writers serving as mentors were William Goldman whose extensive body of work includes *Butch Cassidy and the Sundance Kid* and *Marathon Man* and Terrence Malick (*Days of Heaven, Badlands*).

The meeting with Goldman, which would later become a point of controversy, was little more than a meet-and-greet session, according to Damon. The few suggestions Goldman had didn't fit with the flow of their script.

"As great a writer as William Goldman is, he didn't grow up in Boston," Damon points out. "We set the movie in Boston because that's where we really grew up and that's where we were writing from, from a position of strength. That's one thing we can speak with authority on in a room with William Goldman. 'No sir, they actually don't say that, they say this—and we know that for a fact.' "

However, a meeting arranged with Terrence Malick was more productive and concrete. It was the well-respected writer-director who suggested ways in which Will's love interest, a Harvard medical student named Skylar, could become a catalyst for his decision to leave Boston.

But as the months passed, Matt began to feel as if there would never be an end to the calls for more revisions. The script might have found a home and his bank account might be padded, but Damon realized his movie was no closer to being produced than when before it was sold.

True, some of the delay could be attributed to the fact that both Matt and Ben would go off for acting jobs and not be able to devote themselves full-time to rewrites. But the larger difficulty was inherent in the system itself.

"One of the problems with the Hollywood system is that there are a lot of middle-management people who will say things just to have their presence noted. Then before you know it, you're into six months of rewrites. And when you've invested so much in a script, basically, your whole life, your career, everything is based on getting this movie made and suddenly, *don't worry, just rewrite*."

Even more demoralizing was the growing suspicion that nobody was really paying that close attention to the script anymore. So as a little test, Matt and Ben decided to have some fun. In one particular scene, they added a very crude, non sequitur line that had nothing to do with the rest of the scene. More than anything, it was a joke to see who would catch it first and call them on it.

"But when we handed it in, they made no comment on it. So Ben and I are like, 'Screw this.' "

So for the next story meeting, they expanded the line and added even more explicit dialogue. Again, nobody seemed to notice. Now they really believed their script wasn't being given the attention it needed.

"The montage sequence had grown from one line to three lines and by the end it was almost a paragraph, and they never said anything about it. We thought it would be a little inside joke and when they didn't notice, it was just sad."

With *Courage Under Fire* failing to garner Matt the notice he had hoped it would and with *Good Will Hunting* in development purgatory, Damon kept his spirits up by hanging out with his friends, who were mostly other twentysomething B and C-list actors teetering on the brink of breaking through to bigger and better roles.

"There is a whole group of us that have stuck together for a long time now—it's like Actors Anonymous," he jokes. "That's important because we all go through the same stuff. There were times when I didn't have much money, but I was with a group of actors who were having a similar experience and that made it easier. They didn't have money either, but they had talent. There's a camaraderie about that.

"An actor's life is one based on rejection, even at its highest level; you're never the first choice so I think it helps to have friends who understand the business. You can talk to them and they understand where you're coming from. I can call Cole or Ben anytime and just rap. We do monologues together. We critique each other's work. We're acting-mates. It's what keep us up at night. Late night phone calls. When Ben was filming *Armageddon*, saving the world from an asteroid, he was calling me late at night going, 'There's this scene. What would I say if this happened.'"

Besides Ben, Damon's clique included Cole Hauser, Rory Cochran, Joaquin Phoenix, and Matthew McConaughey, who was the first to make the jump from supporting player to leading man.

"When Matthew got *A Time to Kill* we all went nuts," Damon says, referring to the film based on John Grisham's best-selling book. Almost overnight, McConaughey became Hollywood's new It boy, helped along by his reported romances with his costar, Sandra Bullock. Watching Matthew become a movie poster boy was extremely gratifying to Matt and the others in the group and there was no simmering resentment.

"There was not an envious one among us—it was like we all made it. It was fantastic because he's such a great guy. It was also such a feeling of vindication that one of our peer group, someone not on the A-List, got the part.

It recharged us. I could remember when he was where we still ate, which helped made me believe it could happen for any of us."

When asked why he hadn't felt so vindicated years ago, when after *School Ties* Chris O'Donnell and Brendan Fraser suddenly became hot, Damon considers his answer carefully.

"My relationship with Matthew and Ben is personal. Chris and Brendan, we were friendly when we were working together, but we were never truly close friends. And when something good happens to a friend, it's almost like it happens to you."

About the only thing Matt's circle of friends couldn't empathize with was his frustration over the lack of movement on the *Good Will Hunting* script. He and Ben kept waiting for Castle Rock to finally start showing the script to some top-flight directors, which would be the next step in getting the movie made.

But problems began when Damon and Affleck learned that Castle Rock had not shown the script to any directors, but instead planned to turn it over to Castle Rock partner, Andrew Scheinman. Scheinman's work, the listless *Little Big League*, left Matt and Ben cold. But what really alarmed them was Scheinman's plan to shoot the movie in Canada, and have Toronto double for Boston.

"We felt this movie could be really blundered if it wasn't done properly," says Damon firmly. "Who was going to direct it and where it was going to be shot was really, really important. Because you're walking a fine line with that movie to begin with in terms of making it too sentimental and just making it lame."

The issue of director and location ultimately became the deal-breakers.

Castle Rock's senior executives took what they believed was the high road and rather than force the actors to work with Scheinman, put the project in turn-around. But in reality, what that did was put Damon and Affleck's backs against the wall. Because now they had to find another studio willing to pay the $600,000 Castle Rock had bought the script for *plus* expenses. If they failed, then Castle Rock could do whatever they wanted.

"It was either make it with who they were asking us to make it with or take this risk of trying to sell it else-where," explains Affleck. "We were basically being fired and offered tickets to the premiere of this thing we'd now put three years of our lives into—and it would star someone who wasn't us."

Nor would they be given a lot of time to find another interested party.

"We had thirty days to find someone else or else we were going to have to give it back to Castle Rock and be iced from the movie."

Hollywood translation: Will Hunting would be played by someone like Brad Pitt.

But none of the studios who had bid the first time around were interested during the second go-around because of Ben and Matt's insistence that they star in the film.

"The movie was being sold on two kids nobody knew. They were all like, 'Well, you're pretty much screwed.' So we sat down with Chris Moore, our pro-ducer, and said, 'What are we going to do?' "

What they did was get a little help from their friends. Ben told director Kevin Smith of their studio troubles. Affleck knew Smith from having worked with him on *Mallrats* and most recently, *Chasing Amy*. Smith read the script and thought it would be perfect for Miramax, the renowned independent studio founded by brothers Bob and Harvey Weinstein. Even though the company had passed on *Will Hunting* the first time around, Kevin called Harvey directly, and suggested the script would be a perfect vehicle for Smith's production company.

"When the initial bidding was going on, the script had never gotten to Harvey Weinstein, who's the head— he's God, basically," says Matt. "So Kevin called Harvey and said, 'You have to read this movie.' And that's what got Harvey to read it. Within two days, the deal had been made and we were at Miramax."

Weinstein laid out more than $1 million to Castle Rock for the rights—making it one of the most expensive purchases in Miramax history.

"Had it not been for Kevin Smith we would have lost the film," Damon says. "That's why he's the executive producer of the movie. He did the most important thing that could have happened, which was made sure that it went to Miramax. And the movie would not have turned out the way it did had it not been at Miramax. So we owe a lot to him."

But one incident in particular convinced Matt that his script was finally getting the attention it deserved.

"Ironically, the first thing Harvey said was, 'In that montage . . . you know, I think you might want to take the blow job out. I don't think it fits in with the rest of the film.' "

He knew then they were at the right place.

In December, 1995, Ben and Matt were driving near Needles, California. Matt was still recovering from his weight loss for *Courage Under Fire*, and the two friends were just hanging out and spending some time together. As they were tooling along the deserted highway, they got a call, which Ben took.

The message:

"*You're meeting with Mel Gibson in New York in two days about him directing* Good Will Hunting.

Ben has a pronounced fear of flying and frequently drives crosscountry. So armed with coffee and adrenaline, they drove almost straight through for the next forty-eight hours to get to Manhattan, keeping each other awake by reciting dialogue from Gibson's breakout film, *Mad Max*. Damon remembers the day vividly.

"We got to Miramax's office just before lunch and Harvey tells us, 'Mel Gibson is a great director. You can see that from *Braveheart*.' And I said, 'Harvey, Ben and I have been working. We haven't seen it yet.' So without missing a beat he told us the whole story."

The good news was that a major film star wanted to make their movie. The bad news was Gibson was just about to film *Ransom* and wouldn't be available for almost a year. Damon and Affleck had no choice but to force their hand.

"Mel was really understanding when we said, 'This movie is our life. We know you're like the biggest star in the world but we need a decision.' "

Two weeks later, Gibson withdrew.

But the project wouldn't be without a director for long because at the same time Gibson was withdrawing because of scheduling conflicts, Gus Van Sant was now interested.

Van Sant, who had built a solid reputation with hard-edged films such as *Drugstore Cowboy* and *My Own Private Idaho*, contacted Matt through Casey Affleck, who had worked with Gus on the director's last film, *To Die For*.

"Gus Van Sant knew of us because of Ben's brother," explains Matt. So when we heard he wanted to direct *Good Will Hunting*, we loved the idea because we respected him so much. Gus has this way of delivering earth-shattering news in the most disarming, unflustered flat monotone. 'Yeah, I want to direct. That's if you want to do it. Okay. Bye.'

"So as Ben said, fortune was in favor of us fools."

However, others weren't so sure that Van Sant, an openly gay director whose 1989 masterpiece *Drugstore Cowboy* is credited will revitalizing the American independent film scene, was the best match for the material.

"There were people like Harvey Weinstein who weren't sure I was the right person for this film," Gus freely admits. "I tried to sell myself by saying that *Ordinary People* was my favorite film, which it is. Ben and Matt, however, had faith. Maybe it was harder for the studio executives to make a leap because Hollywood people put you in a category. Ben and Matt never had those preconceptions."

"As an actor," says Affleck, "you see these great performances he gets. He has his own sensibility. We said, 'You're the Indie Guru. It's yours.'"

With Van Sant attached, the script moved into a new phase of development. Instead of a committee of executives each giving their opinions, there was one point man whose job it was to create a vision of the film. The tone, the look, the *feel* of the movie all depended on Van Sant. In some important regards, *Good Will Hunting* became less Matt and Ben's baby.

"The most important step was giving up the script and handing it to Gus and saying, 'This is your movie now,'" agrees Damon. "We had to have a director who was going to heighten it and make it better, otherwise the film would have been a total failure for us."

On any film, the number and kinds of producers varies. In general, an executive producer title goes to the money people. So on *Good Will Hunting* Bob and Harvey Weinberg are listed as executive producers, as are some other Miramax executives. You always know who the executive producers are because they are the people who accept the Oscars for Best Picture. Because Kevin Smith had gotten the script to Weinstein, he was given a co-executive producer credit on the film.

Someone with a title of co-producer, such as Ben's friend Chris Moore was given, can have a number of different duties, depending on the production. Often, they assist the producer, who is the person actually overseeing the day-to-day decision making of a production. It is obviously a position of great power and because the producer deals directly with the cast and director, it is important they are someone who can get along with others.

After purchasing the *Good Will Hunting* script, one of the first things Harvey Weinstein did was look for the right producer to guide the film through development. He chose Lawrence Bender. Bender had started his career as a professional dancer, then decided he could jump-start his acting aspirations via producing. He put his name on the Hollywood map as the producer of Quentin Tarantino's *Pulp Fiction* and *Jackie Brown*. At the time he was approached by Weinstein, Bender was considered one of the hottest independent film producers currently in Hollywood.

"Harvey and I were at the New York Film Critics Awards in January 1996 and we were snowed in," recalls Bender. "And Harvey says, 'You know, I got this great script, *Good Will Hunting*, my favorite script at Miramax. I haven't told anyone about it yet, but I want to bring you in to make this thing.'

"So I read it and it was great. I hadn't met Ben and Matt yet, but there was something about it. It wasn't like this slick, professional script. Sometimes you read a script and it's just a good read. But at the end of the day, there's nothing—you don't have any kind of residual feeling.

"But when you read this script, there was something about it that was very moving. There was a passion. It really hit me at my heart. It was like a piece of gold. So I called Harvey and I was obviously very interested.

"I met with the guys and they were really cool. They were these young, passionate, obviously very talented guys who were really into it. So we went off and during the next year, we worked on the script, in terms of developing it."

However, according to reports from those involved with the production, Damon, Affleck, Bender, and Van Sant weren't always in agreement. At one preproduction meeting, things got so heated between the producer and the director that Van Sant almost got physical.

"You don't have a creative bone in your body," he reportedly screamed at Bender. "I just want to punch you in your face."

What Van Sant wanted, and demanded, was that Bender promise—in front of Matt and Ben, that he would not interfere creatively. Staking out territory.

"Yeah, it happened," reportedly admitted Bender when asked about the incident. "But then it blew over."

Now with the production team in place, Damon and Affleck set about rewriting the script yet again. All they needed was the green light from Miramax. But it would be close to a year before Weinstein would put *Good Will Hunting* on the fast track because, as Van Sant explains, the lack of star status proved to be a snag. That and the reluctance of many studios to invest in what used to be called "smaller" films, regardless of their quality.

"Studio executives can't tell the difference between a beautifully written screenplay and a so-so one because

Matt and Ben attend the Golden Globe awards, which would honor them for their *Good Will Hunting* screenplay. *(Flower Children Ltd.)*

Matt Damon arrives at the Oscars in March 1998. *(Flower Children Ltd.)*

Matt and Ben celebrate their Oscars with fellow winner Robin Williams, who took home the award for Best Supporting Actor.
*(Flower Children Ltd.)*

Matt and Ben arrive at the Oscars escorted by their mothers. *(AP/Wide World Photos)*

Matt Damon and Minnie Driver together in a scene from *Good Will Hunting*. *(AP/Wide World Photos)*

Damon and his then-girlfriend Minnie Driver attend the *Good Will Hunting* New York premiere. *(AP/Wide World Photos)*

As the psychiatrist in *Good Will Hunting*, Robin Williams tries to get through to Damon's troubled Will. *(AP/Wide World Photos)*

Matt with fellow Best Actor Oscar nominees Robert Duvall, Peter Fonda, Jack Nicholson and Dustin Hoffman. *(AP/Wide World Photos)*

Matt and Edward Norton prepare for their roles in *Rounders* by attending the 29th Annual World Series of Poker. *(AP/Wide World Photos)*

Matt and his mother, Nancy, with Damon's
friend and writing partner, Ben Affleck.
*(Flower Children Ltd.)*

they're following the fashion of the times. In the case of *Good Will Hunting*, it's a simple human story that has no particular fashion connected to it. Human dramas over the past ten years have decreased in importance because of the action movie.

"*Good Will Hunting* was probably the best-written screenplay I had ever read," says Van Sant. "We called it a color-by-numbers script: if you just filled in the scenes as they were written, it would come to life. But just because I wanted to do the picture, that didn't make it a go," says the director.

That would only happen after Matt finally got the break he'd been waiting his entire career for.

"We were lackadaisical about it until all of a sudden Francis Coppola cast Matt in *The Rainmaker* and then Miramax said, 'We're going.' A lot of the film is owed to Francis for casting Matt."

# NINE

**While *Good Will Hunting* remained in what seemed to be** endless development, first at Castle Rock, then at Miramax, Matt was still playing struggling, if not starving anymore, actor. He had several near-misses, which in some respects was even harder. While it was gratifying to be in the running, consistently losing out on big roles can chip away at the morale of a young, ambitious actor.

"I auditioned for *Batman Forever* for the part of Robin," Damon recalls. "When they first offered it to Chris O'Donnell, he wanted more money, so they had auditions and I did a screen test for Joel Schumacher."

But O'Donnell and the studio eventually came to terms and he went on to wear the cape and codpiece as Batman's sidekick.

"Then the role in *Primal Fear* came down to between me and Ed Norton," he continues. "And Ed pretty much put a smokin' on me. I lost twenty pounds to audition for *To Die For*, but Joaquin Phoenix got that part."

Partly because he knew *Good Will Hunting* was waiting in the wings and partly because it's not his personality to give up, Damon would recoup after each disappointment and maintain his optimism.

He would also keep abreast of what scripts had been sold to see if there were any parts available for him. Which is why Matt had actually had his eye on the role of Rudy Baylor for a long time. As soon as he knew they were preparing a film version of John Grisham's best-selling book *The Rainmaker*, he believed he would be perfect in the role of the young, idealistic lawyer.

Unlike many English majors who look down their noses at popular writers, Damon was a fan of Grisham.

"Look, every English professor in his heart wants to be John Grisham," he offers. "As arrogant as they can be, they still wish they were John Grisham. And I'm a sucker for him. I've read all his books. I'm one of the ones who goes, 'I'll only read a chapter,' and then five hours later I'm like cross-eyed trying to finish it.

"I knew *The Rainmaker* was the next Grisham project that was going to be made and then I heard Francis Ford Coppola was going to direct it. That's when I told my agent, 'Please, just let me be in the room with him. I'd just be so honored to meet the guy.'"

Damon went in to read, but only for the casting director, not Coppola.

"And afterwards, I kept hearing that he wasn't going to meet anybody, and that he was going to cast it with someone else."

That someone else was Damon's old rival, Edward Norton, who had gone on to make a huge splash in *Primal Fear*, earning an Oscar nomination for his role as the psychotic killer. Early in preproduction, Joanne Woodward was being wooed to play the mother and Sean Penn the shady paralegal and Nick Nolte the insurance company rep. In the end, the roles went to Teresa Wright, Danny DeVito, and Jon Voight.

Disappointed, Matt put *The Rainmaker* out of his mind. But what he didn't know is that the lead role had yet to be firmly decided. Coppola, always an intuitive filmmaker, knew the movie would live or die on the casting of its young male lead. Although Norton would seem a solid, logical choice, Coppola wanted one last look.

"So I got a phone call in the summer of 1996, literally at five P.M. in the afternoon and I was told I would have to be in Memphis the next morning," recounts Damon. "*The Rainmaker* was the first call I got after *Courage Under Fire*. I was in Boston so I ran to Logan airport and I got on a plane.

"I reread the book on the plane and didn't sleep all night. They had faxed me the scenes and I just remember staying up all night and reading the scene over and over again, committing it to memory, and basically doing anything to get this role. But I didn't really have time to prepare so I threw together this kind of haphazard performance."

Which included a southern accent. Damon was convinced the only way he had any shot at all was to prove he could pass for a Tennessee lawyer.

"I got lucky because the girl I was dating at the time was from Texas. I could do her accent so that's what I did. It's different from a Knox County Tennessee accent, but it was close enough."

But Matt believes his biggest stroke of luck was doing his screen test with Claire Danes. Danes first gained attention as the angst-filled teenager in the television series *My So-Called Life* but has gone on to be one of the more respected young actresses in Hollywood thanks to her performances in *Romeo and Juliet* opposite Leonardo DiCaprio and *Les Miserables*.

"I think a big part of it was Claire, because she was my scene partner and it was fortuitous. I think he was going to cast her no matter what because she was clearly the most qualified one for the job. So whoever she had read with would have gotten the part. The actor that was originally meant to get the part, Ed Norton, got sick so I ended up reading with her.

"The truth is, I never thought I'd get the part because normally, if you hear about something on such short notice, then they don't want you. You're just filling space.

"I'm convinced to this day that Francis called Claire and said, 'Do you think we should cast that Damon kid?' " jokes Damon, before adding more seriously, "I never asked Francis but I think he saw *Courage Under Fire* after my screen test and thought, *This kid's obviously willing to beat himself up*."

When he got the news he had been cast, Damon was ecstatic, for more than one reason. First, he knew that *The Rainmaker* could do for him what *A Time to Kill* had done for his good friend Matthew McConaughey. But almost as important to Matt was the knowledge that a starring role in a major film could have a positive impact on *Good Will Hunting*.

"The day after I got *Rainmaker*, I sent Harvey a fax. We'd been trying to get *Good Will* done for a year by then and I said, 'Dear Harvey. I am *The Rainmaker*. I'm that guy,' He called back and said, 'All right. I'll call you.' And he eventually saved the day."

Coppola's gamble on Damon gave him what's referred to as "heat" within the industry and it helped nudge Miramax Films, which had been trying to properly package *Good Will Hunting* and get it into production.

Weinstein was smart enough to know that a John Grisham movie directed by Francis Coppola was going to garner a lot of attention and be a solid box office performer. There would probably be no better time to put the movie on the fast track than right then. Which is what he did. Suddenly, a timetable for *Good Will Hunting* was put into motion and for the first time, the script was truly on the road to being filmed.

But first, Damon had another movie to make. *The Rainmaker* was filmed on location in Memphis from late 1996 to early 1997 and to help prepare for the role, Damon relocated to Tennessee prior to filming. He spent a month in Knoxville, where his character in the movie, Rudy, hails from. Matt tended bar and went to local high school football games so when production began a month later in Memphis, he knew Rudy's Knoxville roots.

"I made some friends and I had them take me to their neighborhoods, to figure out where I was from. It was a great experience."

And one that he now knows may never come again. Matt would later muse that his ability to blend in anonymously like that might be a thing of the past.

"What was great about *The Rainmaker* was when I was bartending, people didn't know who I was. It would have gotten in the way if they knew who I was. So in that sense, if my movies start doing well, my job might get hindered. But I hope I can find a way, 'cause that's what's most important.

"Acting affords you a lot of opportunities. When we did *Courage Under Fire*, Denzel Washington was allowed to lead tank battles. They really gave him command of these mock tank exercises and strategy lessons. I don't think he would have gotten that if he wasn't who he was. So there's a trade-off. And there are worse injustices in the world than my not being able to research anonymously."

Part of the impetus for delving so intensely into the

character was that the preparation helped calm Damon's nerves.

"I was really scared to work with Francis," he admits. "I was scared that I'd let him down, which would have devastated me forever. To have this great director saying, 'You don't have it, kid,' would be devastating.

"I think John Grisham knew I was nervous and he tried to put me at ease. He's a very charming Southern gentleman. He said, 'Just take it easy. You'll do all right.' "

For Grisham, seeing his books turned into high-powered movies was becoming old hat. *The Rainmaker* was just the latest, the others being *The Firm, The Client, The Pelican Brief*, and *The Chamber*. All of Grisham's books tell the story of lawyers caught in extraordinary circumstances.

In *The Rainmaker*, the attorney is recent law school grad Rudy Baylor who is struggling to get his career off the ground in lawyer-filled Memphis when two cases fall into his lap. The first has him handling the will of an elderly woman, Miss Birdie played by Teresa Wright, who wants to leave her imaginary fortune to a televangelist; the other is a lawsuit against an insurance company who refuses to pay for a bone-marrow transplant for a young man dying of leukemia, calling it an uncovered experimental procedure.

Among the many subplots is one that has Rudy become attached to a young abused wife, played by Claire Danes, whose husband has literally beaten her with a baseball bat. But the main focus is the insurance case. His client, Donny Ray Black, comes from a dirt-poor family. His mother works to support the family because the father is brain-damaged.

Because the case is of such importance, Rudy reluctantly turns it over to the disreputable attorney named Bruiser Stone (Mickey Rourke). But when federal agents come calling for Bruiser and he disappears, Rudy finds himself alone in the courtroom, going up against the insurance company's version of the Dream Team, including their unethical leader, John Drummond, played with villainous glee by Jon Voight, who is making a cottage industry of playing sleazy bad guys.

While Great Benefit Insurance's side has a half dozen high-priced, experienced civil attorneys, Rudy has his own inexperience and a staff of one—his ambulance-chasing paralegal Deck Shifflet (Danny DeVito) who has failed the bar exam six times.

So of course, in the end, Rudy wins the case. But not soon enough to save Donny Ray's life.

Coppola changed some aspects of the book, the most notable by doing away with the weak subplot about Miss Birdie's will, leaving that character to be the film's delightful comic relief as Rudy's landlady.

For as important as *The Rainmaker* was to Damon, it was equally as important to Coppola. The director had made two movies that many people consider to be among the best ever made—*The Godfather* parts I and II.

He has also made films that were both critical and box office disasters, such as *One From the Heart* and *Rumble Fish* even though both were creatively innovative.

He had tried to establish his own studio, Zoetrope, but it had gone under. Unlike some of his contemporaries such as Spielberg and Lucas who possess unimaginable wealth, Coppola was not independently wealthy. He still had to work for a living. He was a true Renaissance man, who dabbled in theater, opera, and publishing. He was a vintner, his wines generated a modest business.

Since starting his career in the early 1960s, Coppola has directed nearly twenty films. At his best, Coppola can capture time and place like no other, as seen in films like *Apocalypse Now*, *The Conversation*, *Cotton Club* and *Bram Stoker's Dracula*.

To some, fusing such an iconoclast with a mainstream author like Grisham might have seemed an odd pairing, but according to the director, he thought accepting the assignment to direct the film was simply the best business decision he could make.

He initially became familiar with the book when he saw it in the airport while on his way to a vacation in France. "I saw all these thousands of copies of *The Rainmaker* and I thought, enviously, 'What does this guy know that I should learn? How do you come up with a story that all these people want to read?'

"Frankly, I had never read a John Grisham book before," Coppola admits. "But when I read this one, I liked the characters, who are all sort of zany.

"Danny DeVito plays this guy who flunked the bar exam six times and runs around now like the Artful Dodger through alleyways. And there's this eccentric lady, played by Teresa Wright, who is so lonely that she invents this fortune to get attention. Or Bruiser Stone, (Mickey Rourke), is a guy who is sort of a gangster but is really a lawyer. I loved these characters. They're all unusual and all set in a social drama that's different. There's no serial killer, no Mafia killing anybody, no Russian agent. Nothing fantastic, just people.

"I liked the backdrop and the fact that it was mostly set in offices, where you see people work. I never thought of lawyers in that way—as guys who have to go out and look for jobs to make a buck, who work at get-

ting the job, and then work once they get it. I appreciated that feature.

"I also liked that the book was a best-seller, because
that's an indication it had a story that people were interested in. And I liked the theme of the book, which has
to do with a young person looking at a profession from
one definite perspective. That's what made me really get
into it.

"You know, as a director, they don't pay you to be
creative. You have ideas and they say, 'Well, we don't
know,' or, 'Will you do it for nothing?' They always
exact a price. So it helps when you're dealing with
something that has some personal worth to you, like
this situation," he says.

"So, yes, this film was an *assignment*, but it was one
I was grateful to have because of these elements. And
my goal on this film, given all its great characters, was
to come up with wonderful performances."

Not the least of which was the movie's lead character,
Rudy. Coppola had one specific vision for that role.

"I saw the main character as a knight, helping all the
women in the film—the old lady, the mother of a dying
boy (Mary Kay Place), the insurance woman (Virginia
Madsen) and the girl who's a battered wife (Claire
Danes).

"I purposely cast this character extremely young
because there's an idealism in *The Rainmaker*. The film
is about not selling out, which I think is the opposite of
opportunism. It's what John Grisham's stuff is about.
And there's this Grisham tradition in Hollywood now.
You go into one as a filmmaker saying, 'Okay, I'm
gonna do the best John Grisham movie.' "

Which were Matt's sentiments exactly.

# TEN

**Once filming started, Damon worked tirelessly to make sure** he gave the performance of his life. Not only was he awestruck to be working with Coppola, but Matt was also anxious to measure up to the other actors.

"Mickey Rourke is my hero. He won't do anything on screen if it's not true. There was a scene, which got cut out, where all he had to do was chortle and say his line and he wouldn't. I started telling jokes and they used up eleven minutes of film while I told joke after joke. And if he didn't like my punchline he'd shake his head. Then I'd tell a joke he liked and he'd do the laugh."

While some actors might be a tad annoyed at Rourke's way of working, Damon took it in stride and made a learning experience out of it.

"I love it. It's absolutely honest. It's an actor saying, 'I'm trying my hardest to give the truest emotions. Everything I'm doing is real.' It *can* be indulgent to a degree, though," he acknowledges.

"In most movies it would be his responsibility to come up with the motivation himself to laugh. But Francis gets performances that are more layered and textured because he's willing to wait and give that extra time.

"Francis is very indulgent of actors and very much wants spontaneity, those happy accidents which occur when you're acting. Once I went up to a door and knocked on it. Mary Kay Place was supposed to be at the door, but then some other actor was there instead, so I did a double take. Francis came up to me and said, 'See, you never know who's going to answer a door in my movie.' In other words, wake up and go with what's happening.

"It was a great lesson."

Coppola's way of working appealed to Matt, who enjoyed working under less rigid rules.

"Francis takes the technical side, that burden, off the actor. And he's very generous in that regard. That's a huge thing, to be able to have the freedom to do what you want and be relaxed in a scene that requires a lot of movement. He'll watch you work and then he'll shoot around that. You know, and that's unbelievable. That's a gift.

"Francis also really wants you to try wacky stuff on the set. I'm not kidding. He was constantly trying to keep you on your toes. His theory is that in life you don't know what's going to happen next, so why in a movie should you know you're going to say this, walk there, hit that mark? It should be more spontaneous and unplanned. You would open the door and there would be naked people there. It was nuts."

Whatever the directed wanted to try, Matt was more than willing. His work ethic and overall good attitude once again left a lasting impression on the other members of the production.

"I couldn't believe he was from the North because he had such extremely good manners," Southern-born Pamela Chapman says.

Mary Kay Place is an unabashed Damon fan. "The thing that kills me about Matt is he worked more than anybody in the film, sixteen hours a day for four and a half months. And you never heard him get irritable or complain even though you could see he was exhausted. He's generous beyond belief, both to the crew and the cast.

"I can't say enough good things about him. He had absolute respect for everyone from the craft services people to Francis Coppola. There's no arrogance in him, but he's not the geeky good guy either. There are old-soul qualities in him, with old innocence, and yet he's real street-smart—he's paradoxical in that sense. There's a little edge to him that has to do with his intelligence, and a real generosity of spirit. He has a huge heart, this guy."

There was a virtual love-fest between Matt and then-seventy-nine year-old Teresa Wright. The actress, who won the Best Supporting Actress Oscar in 1942 for her work in *Mrs. Miniver*, was vociferous in her praise of her young costar.

"I can tell you that he's marvelous to work with and he's a great help to other actors. He doesn't have a thought about being a picture star. He's interested in being an actor because he truly loves acting. What makes him interesting is that he listens to other people in any scene.

"He has a great desire to do things that matter to him. *The Rainmaker* seems easy, but it was quite difficult. Matt was in almost every scene. What makes you interested in that character of that lawyer is that his desire to do a good job is a direct reflection of Matt, who has great sincerity behind what he does and tremendous energy."

For Matt, working with someone of Wright's pedigree was like reliving history.

"The best thing I saw happen, the most *profound*

experience on the whole movie, was working with Teresa Wright. I just love this woman. We were standing on the sidewalk in front of a big yellow house used in the movie, and we were talking. This elderly woman walked up and said, 'Miss Wright' and she held out a picture of Teresa Wright signed and dated December, 1942. She said, 'Would you resign this picture?' It was an amazing moment to watch as she pulled out this framed picture with shaking hands that she'd had for fifty-four years of the actress she so admired."

One of the most difficult days of the shoot for Damon came when he had to film the scene where Donny Ray dies. And to him, it was the epitome of why he believes Coppola is one of the finest living directors.

"For that scene, Francis told me he didn't want to me think of anything, just to walk into the room, pull up a chair next to Donny Ray's bed and watch over him. Then Francis started reading passages from a book, about how the uninsured die. And I don't know what happened, it just really got to me probably because I had lost a friend eight years earlier. I was embarrassed, trying to hold it in.

"But after they'd cut and stopped shooting, I just lost it. The Director's Guild was shutting us down for the night because we'd gone overtime and we had to leave. They had already turned the lights off and I was just sitting in the dark bawling my eyes out. Francis ordered everyone back in, turned the lights back on and rolled the camera on me for eleven minutes while I just lost it. It was really hard."

However, it wasn't all work and no play for Damon either. Starting with this film, Matt would begin to earn a bit of a reputation as a leading-ladies man, albeit a sensitive one. During the filming, Damon became briefly involved romantically with costar Claire Danes, who was then only seventeen. But the fling was brief and by all accounts the two parted amicably and remain friends.

However, Damon did leave some tender feelings behind. Another member of the production, assistant casting director Anne-Marie Caskey, says that Matt is one who can turn on the charm, especially if he's after something. Caskey admits she thought Matt had a crush on her. "But then I realized he was just trying to catch on to my Memphis accent."

His flirtations aside, for his part, Coppola believes Damon has the movie world at his feet.

"Actors like Matt are in as good a position as they've ever been. They've become the trademarks of the movies, not the directors. There's barely a movie now that can be made without a Cage or Ford or Pitt. Now they determine what movies get made. Matt has got the gift—and he's a writer in his own right. That gives him something special."

It also gave him a lot of work to do. With *Good Will Hunting* on the Miramax fast track, it was important to get the script worked into shape once and for all. So that meant double duty for Matt while Matt was working on *The Rainmaker*—not only was he acting in one film, he had to work on the script for another in what little spare time he had.

For the most part, the revisions were going well under Van Sant's careful eye, although there were a couple of occasions where Matt and Ben were skeptical of Gus's suggestions. Damon remembers one such incident with particular clarity.

"Gus and Ben came down to Memphis while I was still shooting and as we were working on the script, Gus said, 'I want Chuckie to get killed,' " Matt recalls, referring to the part of Will's best friend which Ben was going to play. " 'I want him to get crushed like a bug at the construction site.'

"Ben and I thought that was a *terrible* idea but Gus thought it'd be really cool. 'It'll be the Act II climax.' We thought it was a *terrible* Act II climax but we wrote a draft of it for Gus anyway, where Chuckie got crushed like a bug.

"Later, when Gus read it, he said, 'It's a terrible idea.' So we threw it out. We probably have it on our computer somewhere. We also have Will getting killed. That was an original ending—to have Carmine come back with his boys and a baseball bat to kill Will, who deep down wants to be killed. It was his way of getting out."

But the point was, Matt and Gus were ultimately on the same cinematic wavelength and all the years of hard work seemed on the verge of paying off.

"It had been five years of a lot of struggling, with very low lows and very high highs," Damon admits.

Van Sant then went about the business of trying to attach a name actor to the film via the part of the psychiatrist, which had been specifically written as a vehicle for some actor of stature. So it was Van Sant who first approached Robin Williams with the script.

Years earlier, the two had tried to develop a film about Harvey Milk, the openly gay San Francisco politician who was shot to death by Dan White. White was eventually acquitted thanks to his "Twinkie" defense—he couldn't be held accountable because all the junk food he ate had addled his mind.

Williams agreed to read the script and says he was blown away.

"I just read this extraordinary script and said, 'I have to be a part of this.' It's the type of thing you'd read and be insane not to do.

"It's a very interesting character. People could compare it somewhat to the character I played in *Awakenings*, but he's much tougher and kind of more damaged than that. It's about a man who has something to teach. When I read it I thought this stuff had so many layers to it and that's why I wanted to do it.

"However, at first I wasn't available to do it but they made it work around my schedule. They said they'd start early."

Bender remembers the day Williams committed to star in the film.

"We had got Robin Williams, we locked the deal. But because of his next movie, we only had five weeks of preproduction. I called up Gus and go, 'Gus, the good news is we just signed Robin Williams. The bad news is, we have to shoot in five weeks and that might mean we might need to make compromises. We may not have the time to find locations and design the movie the way you want to do it. Are you okay with that? If not, let's talk.'

"He said, 'I don't see any problems whatsoever. I don't think we're going to have to compromise.'

"And he was right. That was a big vote of confidence for me because I really didn't know Gus that well and to hear him say that made me go, 'Wow, I'm working with a professional.' Not only is he a great filmmaker, but he's a pro, too. He realized that to be able to bend and change is something you need."

Damon remembers Williams's involvement coming about another way.

"We begged Robin, and I think he really wanted to do it. I also think Robin wanted to work with Gus Van Sant, so we were lucky Gus was involved."

Finally, after two studios, ten drafts, and a more than a few sleepless nights, the script for *Good Will Hunting*

was a go. Weinstein gave the script his stamp of
approval and the next step was to actually film the
movie. What had started as an action thriller was now
a small, personal story.

"Matt plays a genius," explains Ben. "But he's not
reluctant; he's a happy genius. It's kind of like the
Dream Team. We always liked the Dream Team because
they beat everybody by forty points. That's what this
movie is about, a kid who beats everybody by forty
points."

Van Sant sees the movie in more symbolic terms.

"Our lead character learns that we all have reservations about doing something that jeopardizes other
things that we have. The film is saying don't be afraid
to do that. And I think it's something that I run across
every day."

In the final version of the script, Robin Williams plays
Sean McGuire, an understanding therapist recruited to
help a very brilliant young man with some very real
problems. The genius needing the attitude adjustment is
Will Hunting, a night janitor at the Massachusetts
Institute of Technology. He's a tough Boston "Southie"
whose favorite pastime is hanging out with his rowdy,
foul-mouthed Irish-American buddies, who squander
their time participating in barroom brawls and who for
entertainment bully guys from other neighborhoods.
Will's best friend, since childhood, is Chuckie, who
knows of Will's gift and encourages him to use it.

Not only is Will a math prodigy, but he also has a
photographic memory. He can consume encyclopedic
knowledge in a sitting—and it turns out he can work
out solutions to mathematical problems that frustrate
the Nobel laureates at MIT.

Except for his buddies, nobody knows about Will's
abilities, until a brilliant-but-short-of-genius professor,

Lambeau, played by Stellan Skarsgard (the husband in *Breaking the Waves*), offers a prize to any student who can solve a difficult problem. The next morning, the answer is written on a blackboard standing in the hall. Lambeau is both enthralled and envious of Will's capabilities. But recognizing genius when he sees it, he makes overtures to help Will. Perhaps he can get him into the school or collaborate with him. But Will is ambivalent.

However, when Hunting and some of his buddies are arrested after getting into yet another fight, Will avoids going to prison on assault charges when the professor intervenes. There are two specific conditions to his probation. The first is Will must study math with Lambeau at M.I.T. The second is he must go into court-ordered therapy with Lambeau's old college roommate, Sean McGuire, for his violent behavior. The psychiatrist, though, has issues of his own, stemming from the death of his wife two years earlier.

Despite Will's resistance, McGuire and Hunting seem to complement one another. For one thing, the therapist is also a Southie and so he understands the obstacles Will has faced in his life.

Will's life is further complicated by his new love interest, a British pre-med Harvard student named Skylar, played by Minnie Driver. In her own right, Skylar is also a bit of a genius, but unlike Will, she's got her life under control, coming from a wealthy family, with her future set with plans to attend Stanford Medical School.

Much of the conflict in the film comes from the fact that for Will to move on with his life, for him to reach his potential, for him to become a good person, he has to reject not only his old behavior, but his old friends too. Chuckie understands this and lets Will know it's okay.

"You're sitting on a winning lottery ticket. It would be an insult to us if you're still around here in twenty years." In the end, Will does move on and leave his Southie friends behind.

On one hand, *Good Will Hunting* doesn't really cover any new cinematic ground, but what does shine through is Matt and Ben's personal passion for the material. They gave the script a definite sense of time and place and infused the characters with real personality.

# ELEVEN

**Once Robin Williams was set to play the psychiatrist, the** *Good Will Hunting* production moved into high gear. Although they were interested in all aspects of their film, the one area that was especially important to Matt and Ben was the casting process. As actors, they knew the importance of having strong people to work opposite. And as first-time writers, they wanted the talent who spoke their words to be first-rate in order to make their script look as good as possible.

"We never fancied ourselves writers," admits Damon. "And actually, it was a source of embarrassment for us when we sold the script because a lot of our friends really are writers and can write a lot better than we can, except maybe dialogue. Writing a script is different though, because to me it's not really writing. It's acting, is what it is. We still don't call ourselves writers. We just kind of go, 'Well, I guess that worked.' "

But to make their dialogue work the best, they wanted the best talent available. So of course, wherever possible, they suggested friends for roles. It's no coincidence Ben's brother Casey was in the film, playing Morgan, one of Will's townie cronies. Or that Cole Hauser was also hired. But the majority of roles were cast through a lengthy audition process. Perhaps the most important role other than the psychiatrist was the part of Skylar, Will's love interest. As it turned out, the casting would have an important impact on Matt's personal life as well.

Originally, Miramax had wanted Claire Danes for the part of Skylar, but her movie dance card was already filled. At first glance, Minnie Driver might not be the obvious choice to play an American medical school student who falls in love with a janitor prodigy. But it's a testament to the respect Driver commands in the industry, and her talent with accents, that she was called to read with Damon after the casting had been narrowed down to the final few actresses.

The audition was held at New York's Soho Grand Hotel, and when Minnie walked into the room, Matt already knew of her work but was taken aback by her commanding physical presence and undeniable sexuality and beauty. Damon was, quite simply, blown away by Driver. Not only as an actor, but as a man.

"Minnie was just like wow—totally amazing. I mean, we all knew who she was. It was intimidating enough when she walked into the room. Then we started doing this scene in the movie where we get in a huge fight and she did it three times in three different accents. She did it in an English accent, an American accent, and an Irish accent. It was extraordinary in each one."

"Matt wasn't prepared for such powerful acting against him," comments producer Lawrence Bender. "They did a scene where Will tells Skylar, 'I don't love you.' There were five guys in the room and nobody wanted to look at one another because we had tears in our eyes. Matt literally had to stop the audition, apologize, and start all over."

Damon admits he got completely tongue-tied during the audition.

"Finally, she's doing the scene for the third time in this Irish accent. She starts and I totally blank. After four and a half years of trying to get this movie made, I didn't know where I was, who I was, or what was going on. She's standing there with this Cheshire cat smile thinking, 'Would you like to join me in the scene or are you gonna stand there with your tongue hanging out?'

"I was like, 'Uh, can we start again?' All dorky. But she's just tremendous. I couldn't take my eyes off her during the audition. And when she left, it was just clear around the room that we would never get a better actress than that."

Driver, who was twenty-seven at the time, already had a substantial list of film credits on her resume. She had starred in *Big Night*, appeared in *Sleepers* opposite Brad Pitt, and worked with John Cusack in *Grosse Point Blank*. Ironically, she had gotten her first big break as Chris O'Donnell's plump love interest in 1995's *Circle of Friends*.

Like Matt, she was an actor willing to alter her appearance for the sake of a role. Except in the case of *Circle of Friends*, Driver had to gain weight.

"I was definitely not the right actress for the part physically, but the director, Pat O'Connor, saw that I had the capability as an actor," Driver says. "It's in the job description that you can present yourself as something else.

"In Hollywood, if the part is written as 5'6" and blond, unless you're Nicole Kidman or Julia Roberts, they will not see you. They will say, 'You're physically wrong for the role,' instead of thinking that you can transform or deliberately characterize a part."

For Matt, it was just one more thing to be smitten with.

"I just respect someone who will go that extra mile and

make that much of a sacrifice for their work. It was about the same amount of weight, except in reverse. We did talk about it. Although it's not the healthiest thing to do, she's very dedicated to her work and that's beautiful. That's always the first thing that attracts me to somebody, to see them be so passionate about something."

It was obvious to everyone present at the audition that Damon's interest in Driver extended beyond that of coworker. And when she was hired for the role, it wasn't long before it was equally apparent that there was a definite chemistry between the two that had spilled over into their personal lives away from the set.

But Driver initially wanted to play it a little cool. "I just didn't want to get carried away. I wanted to get to know Matt."

Damon respected her feelings and did his best to downplay the fact that they had begun dating.

"We were trying to keep everything under wraps because I never wanted to take anything away from her performance, which is tremendous. The last thing I would want is for anyone to misconstrue it, to think she got the part because we were going out. She didn't. We met for the first time at the audition."

Beside his personal feelings for her, Matt was also counting on Driver to smooth out the rough edges of Skylar.

"The character of Skylar, I'm sure you can see, is kind of a device," explains Matt. "At least, it certainly read a lot more that way on the page than how it appears on the screen. I mean, we're two guys so how are we going to write a female character? It's really tough to do. It's like writing down stuff girlfriends have said to us and stuff from stories. And then we give it to the best actress we could find and said, 'Please do whatever you want with it.'

"And with that freedom, a great actor can find the right moments and bring something to the confines of that role. Robin Williams is like that too.

"Min is just an extraordinary actress, she's like the best actress I know. Everything from ideas to 'Let's do this' to the rehearsal process, it was amazing just to watch her work."

Driver enjoyed being given free reign on the character, something British film actors are more used to than American movie stars. More and more, American films are heavy on action and light on content, a fact Driver is very familiar with, having worked in the action-adventure film, *Hard Rain*, with Christian Slater and Morgan Freeman.

"That was my foray into the action genre—which I could probably live without. Oh, I read for *The Lost World*, don't think I didn't! Four women read for that part and I was standing there right next to Julianne Moore. But only if it's something like that. There are just some movies that are so absurdly bad. I mean, I read the script for *Anaconda* and was just laughing hysterically.

"What you'd like is to be in a film that does both. *Good Will Hunting*, for instance, has the chance to make a good deal of money. You'd like the film to make money in the right way."

What was more important to Minnie was the chance to show her stuff in a quality, mainstream film. After trying on several accents, Driver eventually settled on using her own in the film. "It was a good way of creating a cultural gulf between my character and Will's.

"Being the girl in these groups has meant that I've been allowed to do whatever I like. Because they've said, 'We've never got her quite right. We need you to fill in the blanks,' the boys let me do what I thought needed to be done, so I got to explore exactly how interesting and dangerous it is to define yourself by another person.

"Skylar does what we would like to believe we can all do. She doesn't shy away, she doesn't run from how hard it is, she opens herself up. I think it's the course that a lot of women would like to believe they could take."

As is typical in films, Driver was the only featured female actress in the movie. But again, she had no problem as the lone women in an all-boy's club.

"I'm so used to being surrounded by men on films. I'm very comfortable in the company of men. I went to a coeducational school where there was absolutely no division between boys and girls. I had it ingrained from a very early age that there was no difference. Actually, though, I find it strange to keep being cast as the object of men. I'm dying to do films with women."

To many outside observers, it might seem fortuitous for the leading man and his on-screen love interest to be involved off-camera, if for no other reason than to bring that personal chemistry to the screen. But director Gus Van Sant was more cautious in assuming the movie would benefit from Damon and Driver's personal attraction to one another.

"There's a rosiness that comes through, but that can be deceiving," comments Van Sant. "A lot of times if you are told something before you see the film, you might convince yourself something's there when it actually turns out to be the opposite."

But if Van Sant was worried during the shoot, he didn't show it. When filming finally started, he was completely focused on bringing *Good Will Hunting* to life. And neither Damon nor Affleck will ever forget the first day on the set. Even though they weren't scheduled to act that initial day, Matt and Ben were among the first to arrive.

"We showed up like, '*Hey, we wrote this,*'" laughs Matt.

"Yeah," adds Ben, "which in Hollywood is like, '*You're the writer? Good. Now you just want to stand away from the action.*'"

Affleck brings up an interesting point. Film is a director's medium so most screenwriters are treated like so much of a nuisance once filming starts. This is one reason many writers also turn to directing, in order to maintain a semblance of control on their screenplays.

But *Good Will Hunting* was a special situation. And Gus Van Sant was a different kind of director. He knew the history of the script and knew how much of their lives Matt and Ben had put into it. So more so than normal, they were included in the process, from the first day on.

That said, Matt is quick to say he and Ben understood their role.

"Despite the fact that Gus is a very communal director in that he wants everyone's opinions, which makes you feel you're part of the team, there can only be one chef in the kitchen when it comes to making a movie," Damon says definitively.

"Movies are the last great dictatorship. They need that. They need a strong voice and a decisive voice and the director is that voice so Ben and I were very conscious of our place—as actors—when it started."

But on the first day of filming, their professional detachment dissolved as they watched Robin Williams and Swedish actor Stellan Skarsgard, who played the professor, in the movie's first take.

"It was amazing. Ben and I went down there just to see Robin say our words," Matt recalls. "We were sitting there and they said, 'Let's roll camera. Sound. Speed. Scene forty-one, take one. Marker. Action.'

"And by the time they got to *action* tears were just running down my face. I just couldn't believe it. Then Robin started to talk and I looked up at Ben and he's crying too. It was really a profound moment for me. I mean, it represented five years of our lives. And it would not have happened if Robin didn't do it.

"After the scene, Robin looked over, saw us and got up. He walked across the whole room and put his hands right on our shoulders and said, 'It's not a fluke. You guys did it. You guys did it.'

"For a guy that classy to do that, it was pretty amazing."

Chris Moore remembers that the cast and crew began applauding Damon and Affleck.

"There was this meaningful moment when Matt and Ben realized, we are making this movie and that is Robin Williams standing over there saying lines we wrote."

Although he has been a successful comedian and actor for years, the moment wasn't lost on Williams, who appreciated what that first scene represented to the two friends.

"They had this dream a long time ago and it was finally happening. It's a lot to take in."

For as emotional an experience as it was, Matt didn't have much time to dwell on it because he had a movie to shoot. Even so, he consumed every aspect of *Good Will Hunting*, intent to learn as much as he could from the people around him. One of his greatest teachers turned out to be Robin Williams.

"Robin could have done anything and we would have been happy for the help, but he stuck very closely to the script and was very respectful of it," Matt says, sounding somewhat awed.

Williams brushes aside the compliment and lobs it back to Matt.

"The truth is, the thing is so good it didn't need me to improvise. The writing was so strong it doesn't need anything. And it's amazing to be working with the person who wrote it.

"There's an emotional core to *Good Will Hunting* that came from Ben and Matt. They have this unspoken twins thing. They care for each other, yet they bust on each other. And that was a great base line to work with. I'm very proud of this movie. It has a resonance."

# TWELVE

**Matt has always used the opportunity of working with other** actors as a chance to absorb their knowledge and experience. One of the things about Williams that most impressed Damon was Robin's ability to so effortlessly mask his natural comic bent.

"It holds Robin back being the funniest man in the world. People really don't give him the credit he deserves as an actor. I think a lot of people think of him as this funny man who channels, where he's actually this person who works extraordinarily hard.

"Robin is very serious and intense in this role and that's how he was when the camera was rolling but once the camera cut, he was the Robin Williams you see all the time, running around the room doing his stuff and making everybody laugh. Luckily, he found a way to marry the two, where he can play the dramatic role, but not at the expense of his comedy.

"And he can still infuse it. There are some jokes in there that really work that are just Robin because he's got that quick mind and just throws them out.

"For example, in the scene where we're talking about his wife, we couldn't keep a straight face. Robin just started improvising. Where he says, 'My wife used to fart in her sleep,' is not what we wrote.

"Gus cuts to me and I start giggling, then cuts back to Robin and he starts giggling. In one of the takes I said, 'That's not what killed her, is it?'

"In this role in particular, he's got the best role of both. Granted, it wasn't an all-out chance for him to do his comedy, but I can't imagine a better performance from anybody."

Damon says one of his biggest thrills was sitting in on the process of scoring the movie. "I went down to the scoring stage and watched Danny Elfman, and that was the experience of a lifetime to not only sit with him at the master board but he let me go into the recording hall and stand next to the conductor. It was like this sixty-five piece orchestra. It was unbelievable. The music just comes right at you, washes over you. It was unlike anything I'd ever experienced. It was awesome," he says, using one of his favorite superlatives.

Damon also has nothing but praise for director Van Sant.

"Gus is a very quiet, reserved director, and he really kind of inspires creativity around him. He just really creates an environment where everyone feels good about their work, and in that environment everyone can do their best.

"I think it's better because there are some directors who are like, 'Move your f---ing ass!' and they're really hard to work for because you're constantly like a cowed dog. But most directors are usually pretty good about involving, if you ask to be involved. It doesn't mean you'll have decision-making powers, but it does mean that you can at least have the director's ear.

"Gus is just very nurturing of what's going on. So, as a result, literally five heads of departments came up to me at the wrap party and said, 'I've never had a movie that was this much fun,' in terms of the experience.

"And it was because of this environment that he created. And so, to get up every day and not only be going into that environment, but going into that environment to say the words that you wrote and that you've been trying to get made for four and a half years was doubly rewarding."

The admiration society was mutual.

"Matt has a great face, so that's always good," Van Sant notes. "But what makes him appealing is he's bringing a character to life so specifically it's mesmerizing."

Damon laughs when told this.

"Come on, this was our daydream. I'm not going to write myself as an asshole." Then on a more serious note says, "I'm not afraid to be emotional. I think that's a key to this film. It touches themes of loyalty and friendship. It's a bit of a welcome change because it's not cynical at all.

"*Good Will Hunting* is about engaging in life, going out and living every day. That's a philosophy I've always had about acting. There are a lot of times when I look back on things I've done, when I really tried my best, and they're embarrassing. Hey, that happens. But I think the worst thing in life is to look at yourself and say, 'What if? What if I'd just taken that opportunity more seriously?' "

One of the things that Matt was most anxious to see come alive on film was the movie's uncredited co-star— the city of Boston.

"No one has ever accurately played a Boston accent, much less the cultural aspects of the city," Damon claims. "Actors start doing a weird Kennedy/Brahmin thing. Robert Mitchum came close in *The Friends of Eddie Coyle*. You've got to be from there to do it. I don't even think Meryl Streep could do it."

Accents aside, it was the city dynamics that Damon wanted to see portrayed accurately.

"I grew up in Cambridge. A lot of the themes of this movie are wrapped up in that upbringing Ben and I had—raised in a middle-class family in a working-class neighborhood with these two esteemed universities—Harvard and MIT—on either side.

"Class, I think, is the heart of prejudice. That's where *Good Will Hunting* came from—how people look at each other and the presumptions made.

"Apparently, some people don't really care for the title, but we liked it. It kind of had that fairy tale aspect, and we thought of it as a fairy tale. We wanted to make Will's gift almost fairytale-like, so that the dichotomy would be more realized in the story. It's about the conflict of class and people being judgmental.

"A lot of things were important to us writing this script: just treating people nicely, not having regrets in the world, being responsible in your relationships and the way you treat other people. That's our philosophy—basically the Golden Rule."

Despite his familiarity with the subject matter, Damon says the screenplay isn't exactly autobiographical, although: "Well, I am a genius," he laughs.

Affleck corrects him. "All of us put together aren't a genius. But it is drawn from our own experiences. The characters are amalgams of people we knew. I don't think we were good enough to totally invent things."

When asked how they wrote some of the film's more moving speeches, which smacked of maturity far beyond their ages, Damon and Affleck confessed they had borrowed from the wisdom of others.

"Some of the speeches were a combination of things, not the least of which were speeches which had been thrown our way by our parents.

" 'Don't think you understand everything already because you don't.'

"And even if we don't understand those things, we understand them enough to repeat them," Matt laughs.

Because mathematics plays such a crucial role in the movie, Damon also wanted to make sure the technical side of the film passed scrutiny.

"If you go through anything point by point, you can pretty much sound smart. It was essentially just doing that—go through the source and try and make an impressive little chunk of dialogue.

"But all of the math stuff in the film is true," he says. "Once the movie was going, we met with MIT professors and professors from Toronto. We had a technical advisor who was a professor who also played a bit part in the movie who helped us with all the equations and all that."

Because Matt had always been a serious student of the business of making movies, he was aware that filmmaking was a business with financial bottom lines and deadlines and accountants counting beans. But on the set of *Good Will Hunting*, Matt was amazed at how those concerns were largely kept at bay and how the production team kept faithful to the spirit of the script.

"Often there's a sense of the clock is ticking, money's being spent—perform right now. And that's antithetical to the entire process of acting, which I think comes out of relaxation.

"But when it takes an hour and a half to set up the lights, I think even with the great actors, when there are lights surrounding you, you feel this pressure to perform. You've got to do something and you can't just play subtle and small, because why would they have bothered to set up all the lights?

"However, we had a great director of photography,

Jean-Yves Escoffier, who is brilliant working with natural light. Jean uses the neon light of a beer sign and you're really in a bar doing the scene so you feel that you can be as comfortable as you are in real life."

More than anything, *Good Will Hunting* was a fantasy come true for two childhood friends who used to plot during lunch how they would one day have Hollywood at their feet.

"I don't think our writing the movie was as ambitious or planned as people make out. We were just desperately trying to have a voice, any voice. We were auditioning for movies that we would not necessarily like or be proud of, but we needed the money and we needed the work.

"Ben and I were pinching ourselves everyday," Damon acknowledges. "This had been such a long road for us and to look over and see your best buddy on the set every day is just an amazing feeling. We hang out together when we're not working, so to look over and see Ben on the set was great.

"Also to watch his work. There was a scene that got cut out of the movie that was he and Minnie. To walk alongside the camera with headphones on and listen to his work, he's just a tremendous actor. He's the best young actor in the world, I think, for my money. Without a doubt. To watch him do his thing was a learning experience for me. And pretty fun."

Damon admits one of the biggest lessons he learned having his script filmed was to better respect a screenwriter's words.

"It taught me a lot about writing, in terms of not wanting to step on another writer's words," Matt admits. "I can now imagine what it feels like for a writer when you start improvising like a madman on the set. Like Ben.

"Kevin Smith always called him 'King of the Mad-Libs' because on *Chasing Amy* Ben would just go into these whole tangents of dialogue and Kevin would have to go, 'Just stick to the f---ing script!'

"I think both of us are more aware now what it feels like to really put yourself out there in terms of writing a script and really having something you want said in a certain way."

Even by himself. Although Damon has no noticeable accent, he had grown up hearing the South Boston cadences and worked hard to maintain a consistent accent throughout the film. In keeping with his perfectionism, Matt pleaded with Van Sant to let him loop dialogue because the Boston accent wasn't just right. Damon ended up redoing it three times until it met with his personal approval.

When the shooting finally wrapped, Matt was beset by conflicting emotions. First and foremost he felt confident that the final film would reflect his original intention for the movie.

"Absolutely. Of course, it's seen through Gus's eyes, so it's always going to be different. But it's either going to be different through a guy like Gus Van Sant's eyes or it's going to be different through some other guy's eyes and obviously we would rather it was Gus.

"All actors want to work with Gus Van Sant. He always has a great idea as to where to put the camera and he gets good performances out of the actors. He rehearses them, then very calmly decides where to put the camera, in a very unobtrusive place. It's just amazing. I felt like my acting was matured by him. I would very much like to work with him again."

Tellingly, Damon did not heap the same compliments on producer Lawrence Bender. Van Sant cut Bender's cameo out of the film, although according to Bender, it was his idea to scrap his role.

"Actually, Gus wanted to keep it in," said Bender. "And I was saying, 'You know what? We don't need it.' So my actor's cap was like, 'Damn man, tell that damn producer to leave me in,' and the producer is saying, 'We don't need this scene.' "

In any event, there's no denying Bender's relationship with the others remained strained throughout the filming. Consider what one of the film's participants would say later, not for attribution.

"The first thing on screen is a Lawrence Bender production. It makes me want to puke."

But during the making of any film there will be personality conflicts, most of which are forgotten—especially if the film becomes successful. What was more unusual about *Good Will Hunting* was the amount of, well, good will, generated during the production.

Anyone looking for a downside would be hard-pressed to find one, although in some later press conferences and interviews, some critics wondered aloud if Ben didn't feel as if he was somewhat playing second fiddle to Matt.

"When you see the movie from the outside you think, 'This is the main guy and this is the supporting guy.' But it was such a collaborative effort that it doesn't bother me. I just wanted to do interesting stuff and stop spending movies slamming high school kids up against lockers."

The reality was, there was nothing that could detract from the enormous sense of accomplishment both Matt and Ben felt once the movie was a wrap.

"This film was many, many years of work," Affleck says. "Whether it's successful or fails, I want to take the victory lap now, just to say, 'Hey, at least we did it: we wrote it, we set it up, we did what we wanted to.' It's a movie I'm proud of."

Damon was slightly more sentimental in his assessment.

"There's a little sadness there," he said, referring to the film's completion. "I'll never have a job that was that much fun, ever, and I realize I'm not going to get up and go to work with Gus and Robin and Ben and Minnie.

"But at the same time, it feels good to have the movie done. I don't think I could ever tire talking about it."

That last sentiment would be put sorely to the test in the months to come.

# THIRTEEN

**It was as if Matt had suddenly turned into an acting** Midas—everything he touched seemed to be turning to gold. His run of good fortune that had begun with *The Rainmaker* was still accelerating. For the guy who had gone six months without a call after *Courage Under Fire*, Damon was now lining up the next job before the current job was even finished.

And the next role happened directly as a result of *Good Will Hunting*.

"It was serendipity," says Matt. "Robin Williams was in Boston rehearsing for *Good Will Hunting* when Steven Spielberg came to the State House in Boston for a day of filming on *Amistad*.

"Robin asked me, 'Do you want to meet Steven?' Well, of course I did!"

"Steven was shooting on the Commons, so we went over and said hello," recalls Williams, who knew the director from when they worked together on *Hook*, Spielberg's remake of the Peter Pan story. "That was the first time he saw Matt."

Damon was thrilled to meet Steven. Not only because he was a great fan of the director's work, but because he also knew that Spielberg was shooting a new film starring Tom Hanks. A film that had a role that was perfect for Matt.

Damon recounts their conversation:

"He said, 'Do I know you? Are you the guy from *Courage Under Fire*?'

"And I said yeah.

"He said, 'Did you gain some weight?'

"The thing is, I had auditioned by tape for *Saving Private Ryan*, but Steven was under the impression I still looked like I did in *Courage Under Fire*. He didn't realize I had lost forty pounds for that job and didn't always look like a skeletal junkie. So when he actually saw me, he saw that I didn't look that way anymore and that's what made the difference.

"A week later, I had that movie. I would never have had access to Steven Spielberg except for Robin Williams. And I never would have had access to Robin Williams except for *Good Will Hunting*."

Because Matt only appears in the final third of the movie, much of *Saving Private Ryan* was filmed when Damon was still working on *Good Will Hunting*. So while Matt was enjoying clam chowder and the company of Minnie Driver, the rest of the Spielberg cast was knee-deep in European mud.

"I was going to get one of those disposable cameras," recalls Damon. "I thought I would take a bubble bath and order champagne and a cigar, and I was going to sit in the bathtub saying, 'Hope the rescue's going well. Love, Private Ryan.' Just to piss them off a little bit."

The movie is a period piece, set in the middle of World War II.

"It's about these four brothers who all go off to fight in the war," explains Damon. "Three of them die in one week beginning with D-Day and there's one surviving brother behind enemy lines. That's Private Ryan.

"The movie is about Tom Hanks and a group of handpicked rangers who are going back to find this guy on what is essentially a political mission, because the government does not want this fourth brother to die. And everyone's grumbling the whole time about how they have to save this kid. Private Ryan, my character, eventually stands for everyone's chance to go home.

"The film starts with D-Day and Tom Hanks going on Omaha Beach, and Steven says it's the best stuff he's ever shot," reports Damon. "I think it will be pretty impressive looking. I'm like, 'Wow, that must have been great for Tom Hanks. Too bad I wasn't there.' "

Whenever possible, Matt likes to feel as if he's walked in the shoes of his character before starting work, but in the case of *Private Ryan* his usual method of research wouldn't work since there was no World War to observe. So he did the next best thing and found a book written by famed World War II journalist, Ernie Pyle, who ultimately died in combat.

"I read *Brave Men*, true accounts of people in combat in World War II, everyone from airborne to infantry," explains Damon.

Although his character is only in the final third of the movie, Damon knew full well that it would be a high-profile role and in a way, a bit of insurance. Even if neither *The Rainmaker* nor *Good Will Hunting* made a splash, he could be assured *Saving Private Ryan* would, thanks to the Hanks-Spielberg combination.

After *Good Will Hunting* wrapped, Damon made his way to England, where Spielberg was filming his movie. Fortuitously, Driver was also scheduled to work on her own period piece, called *The Governess*. So over the summer of 1997, the two lovers were able to spend time together between their shooting schedules.

However much a grown-up man in love Damon was

when he was with Minnie, once he got on the set of *Saving Private Ryan*, he turned into a kid again. So needless to say, he found a playmate in Spielberg.

"When I first met him on the set, he said, 'Hey, you want to see a movie I made when I was fourteen? This is my first war movie.'

"And he shows me this movie and it's got over the shoulder dolly shots. And I'm sitting there watching this thing and said, 'Wait a minute . . . ' and he said, 'Yeah, I used that in *Raiders of the Lost Ark*.'

"It all made sense to me at that point. The guy was editing the movie while he was shooting it. It's just impossible to shoot a movie of that scale that way—and yet he does.

"I think that's what the challenge is now for him. To do it all in one really complicated shot. That's what inspires him now. Because he's done everything. He had the biggest moneymaker, the Oscar-winner, so it's what keeps him going. He's just a prodigy."

Having worked now with two directors whose films have won the Best Picture Oscar, Damon reflected on the differences in style and focus between the men.

"Steven Spielberg and Francis Ford Coppola are both geniuses. But Steven is the exact opposite of Francis. Coppola is very indulgent of the actor and the *actor's process*. Whereas with Steven, it's about his movie.

"However, Steven is very inclusive. He'll get the actors together and say, 'See, this is what we're gonna do. It's gonna be a really cool shot.' It's kind of like being in a group of kids who stole their father's camera and have to get it all in one scene.

"Steven was awe-inspiring to watch. I used to follow him and just shake my head and laugh. I couldn't believe he could do what he did. He knows exactly what he wants and he shoots it so fast and the shots are gorgeous.

"Spielberg is extraordinary," Damon sums up, using his favorite compliment.

Although Steven enjoyed and responded to his young star's enthusiasm, not everyone on the movie knew who Matt was. And his anonymity caused at least one actor some nervousness. When Matt met Dennis Farina on the set of *Private Ryan*, Damon went into his habit of quoting lines from other actor's movies, in this case, *Midnight Run*. However, Dennis didn't realize Matt was an actor in the film and mistook him for some weird fan and was backing away the whole time Matt was reciting the dialogue.

But even that couldn't dampen Matt's spirits. He was flying too high to let the fact that he was still largely an unknown even to most other actors bother him.

"It was the chance of a lifetime to work with Spielberg and Mr. Hanks. Unbelievable. And I've already predicted *Saving Private Ryan* to win Best Picture next year," Damon jokes. "I can say that because I'm not in most of it."

When he got back from Europe in the early autumn of 1997, Matt finally had a moment to reflect on the past extraordinary twelve months.

"I couldn't have had a more amazing year of experiences if I'd dreamed them up. I think Francis's taking a chance on me was a huge factor in getting *Good Will Hunting* rushed into production. And because we were doing *Good Will* in Boston when Steven was shooting *Amistad*, Robin went over to see him and dragged me along. I'm just on a roll."

And the ride was about to get even wilder. In the summer of 1997, few people outside the industry knew who

Matt Damon was. Within a matter of three months, that would all change. His smiling face would grace the cover of countless magazines and become familiar to everyone from serious film-goers to pre-teen girls.

But the Moment of Matt Damon didn't happen by sheer serendipity, as much as the actor might have wished it had. The mass-marketing of Matt Damon was a carefully orchestrated publicity campaign aided and abetted by a few select entertainment editors always looking for the Next Big Thing.

"I want the *New York Times* Arts and Leisure section, *GQ, Esquire* and *Vanity Fair*," explains Chris Pula, a marketing expert who has worked at such high-pressure places as Warner Brothers and New Line Cinema. "Those are the four backbone things that all the press reads that's important in creating a buzz."

Buzz. It used to be that was simply the sound of an annoying insect. Now it's the sound of money. The bigger the buzz about an actor and their upcoming movie, the better the chances are of reaping bigger financial rewards.

A buzz can be generated organically, such as what happened with *The Full Monty*, a small film that caught the fancy of the public without the help of a multi-media publicity blitz. Or it can be manufactured by a few well-placed articles and plenty of hype. In Matt's case, it was a game-plan. It was *must see movie,* as pervasive and shameless as NBC's self-aggrandizing Must See TV campaign.

In February of 1997, Damon's publicist, Jennifer Allen at Hollywood's publicity powerhouse PMK, met with Jane Sarkin, *Vanity Fair*'s features editor. Think of it as a pitch meeting, except instead of scripts and movie ideas being offered, clients are.

The two women talked about several possible story subjects and Allen mentioned Matt Damon. Sarkin had already heard some buzz on him—relatively unknown actor makes good by selling script—so she agreed to feature him in a two-page spread in the magazine's October issue.

Considering that Damon was mostly an unknown commodity, this in itself was quite a coup. But months later, after Editor-in-Chief Graydon Carter was shown scenes from *The Rainmaker* and *Good Will Hunting*, he moved Damon back for the December cover. It was an almost unheard of turn of events. Almost, but not quite. A similar push had occurred with Damon's friend Matthew McConaughey two years earlier just prior to the opening of *his* John Grisham film, *A Time to Kill*.

When suggested he might follow in the footsteps of his friend Matthew McConaughey, Damon waved off the idea.

"That would suck. I don't know if I'd necessarily like the publicity, but I'd love the doors it would open."

But once word was out that *Vanity Fair* was so hot on Damon as to give him a cover, others quickly jumped on the editorial bandwagon. After that followed a *Time* magazine feature and an interview with the *Los Angeles Times*. Once the ball was rolling, every entertainment editor worth his salt didn't want to be left out of the loop.

"The business is now driven by movie stars," explains Damon's agent, Patrick Whitesell. "More and more the studios need leading men to hang their films on. And once you've gotten past Tom Cruise, Brad Pitt, Matthew McConaughey, Keanu Reeves, who is there? There's a real need for more leading men. It's a supply-and-demand thing."

*Vanity Fair* understands that, which is why they load their covers with leading men, such as Brad Pitt, Ralph Fiennes, and Leonardo DiCaprio.

What made the hoopla about Matt Damon so surreal was that the average reader and movie-goer, not to mention editor and journalist, had no idea whether or not Damon's movies were any good or whether Matt himself would prove charismatic enough to warrant the movie star attention and treatment he was receiving. The media frenzy was based solely on buzz.

Ben Affleck, for one, had definite feelings about the value of buzz. "You know what you can do with buzz? Do you know how many movies, just before they come out, have 'great buzz' and then no one goes to see them? They bomb and the people who were involved in the movie go home, saying, 'But we had great buzz.'

"If someone tells me, 'I hear your movie is great!' then I ask them did they see it and they tell me, 'Oh, no, but a friend of mine told me it was great.' That means absolutely nothing. Now, if you tell me you saw it and really liked it, that's another story. But 'buzz' in the end is worthless."

However, the buzz humming around Damon was twofold. In part, the movies were being promoted because Matt would talk about them. But the buzz set into motion by Jennifer Allen was directed specifically at her client. *The Rainmaker* and *Good Will Hunting* would benefit by their association with him, not the other way around. It was placing the personality before the work—a concept that made Damon, a champion of the work process, more than a little uncomfortable.

"It's just weird to think about all that. It still feels so fabricated," he admitted in one interview. "First of all, not that many movie-goers have seen me yet so it doesn't feel real.

"No one has bought a ticket for either of these movies yet. It's only the media and I keep getting the feeling that we've all gotten together to rock the general public. It feels like it could all go away so it's absolutely a lot of pressure. It's very scary. Honestly, the anxiety level is very high."

Even for someone as grounded as Damon, being in the eye of the storm is a dizzying experience. For once, it was a situation that Ben couldn't really help him with because he was going through a similar adventure, although to a much less intense degree. So Damon turned to someone who would know because he had been there himself and asked Matthew McConaughey for advice.

"He's an extraordinarily positive guy with an amazing take on the world. He was a good person to talk to about it, because he won't get affected by any of the nonsense."

McConaughey's advice? *Enjoy the ride.*

*The Rainmaker* and *Good Will Hunting* were scheduled to open within weeks of each other between late November and mid-December, so by Thanksgiving 1997, Matt seemed to be everywhere. On their December issues, subscribers to *Vanity Fair* saw a well-scrubbed Damon smiling back at them, posed in a bathtub with a toothbrush in his mouth. He looked all of eighteen.

"It is strange to see yourself on the cover of a magazine," Matt admits. "Especially when the magazine comes out before the film because in a lot of ways, you feel like you haven't earned it. So now I'm on the cover of a magazine with a toothbrush in my mouth. So to get recognized I have to walk around with a toothbrush in my mouth."

Unlike some actors who quickly get tired of answering the same questions over and over in interview after interview, Matt remained unfailingly polite. Partly because that's who he is, and partly because it really did seem as if he could talk about *Good Will Hunting* forever and not get tired. But he was aware that the marketing end of the business had little to do with his craft and nothing to do with his art.

"That's not what I signed up to do. This shameless self-promotion is antithetical to acting. That's what I do. I'm just looking forward to getting back to work."

If Matt was uncomfortable being the Next Big Thing, his mother was beside herself. As a lifelong, unapologetic, way left-of-center promoter of the common good, the marketing of her son felt like a betrayal.

"I'm not happy about it, particularly. He's a product and people use him," says Nancy Carlsson-Paige bluntly. "I hadn't seen *Vanity Fair* before. I was so shocked—hundreds of pages of advertisements for things nobody needs. This is unbelievable. My beautiful boy is on the cover, really at some level he's being used to sell the products. It's not a healthy relationship.

"Here is an artist and he's just a cog in the capitalist system. He's not a human being anymore. He's become a product people can pick up and judge. It's so out of the ordinary that I worry he might not grow as I want him to.

"What happens in a consumer society is that people become objects of attention in a way that doesn't seem healthy to society. I'm happy that Matt is happy in his work, but I'm not convinced he has to be on the cover of a magazine about it. It's a little hard for me to accept.

"And whether he's good or bad, they'll put him away and pick up another product anytime now. I feel bad about that. I worry about that—how will it affect him."

Others more familiar with the experience of being deluged with sudden fame seemed less concerned about how Matt would ultimately cope.

Robin Williams acknowledges that both Matt and

Ben were far more mature in their dealing with the attention than he had been when he suddenly burst into national consciousness as a wacky space alien in the television series, *Mork and Mindy*.

"The amazing thing when you see them is how grounded they are compared to me. When fame hit me, it was like body-surfing in a typhoon. I was like, 'Well, this is certainly fun and I might have actually made that phone call,' but it was so surreal and it was also frightening. And they are so calm with it. Calm and adult—and Buddhist."

Gus Van Sant, who had worked with River Phoenix in *My Private Idaho* and saw how fame had helped destroy him, is more philosophical.

"If Matt's not ready, then probably nobody's ready. And in some ways, nobody is ready. You can't really escape unchanged in some way. But I think he's had a lot of experience in the business. He's worked with a lot of different people, so hopefully if it makes him mean, he'll recognize it."

In the end, Matt was able to rectify being used as marketing bait because he didn't let the buzz cloud the most important thing: at the end of the day, when his celebrity faded, he would still be an actor and that's what was most important to him.

"Either way, I'm happy with my work. I gave it my all, so if it doesn't work, I have no regrets. The biggest change in my life is that I know I'm working until October, which is fantastic—and daunting. Other than that, I'm still a twenty-seven-year-old punk."

A twenty-seven-year-old punk now making over half a million dollars a film, despite the majority of the public not knowing who the hell he was. And as often happens, Matt was too busy working to actually be able to kick back and enjoy spending any of that money.

"I haven't had much of a life this year because I've been on the road working," he says. "I haven't lived anywhere since Ben and I got rid of our New York apartment. He was there for two weeks last year and I was there for five days and we paid rent for the whole year. It was crazy.

"Ben's now living with his girlfriend in L.A. and I just finished working on *Saving Private Ryan* so I'm going to stay with my friend Cole Hauser. I'm homeless in the best sense of the word. I've got three bags that I've been carrying around with me for over a year, since last August when I got *The Rainmaker*."

Other than what he could stuff in those three bags, the rest of his belongings were in a Jersey City, New Jersey, storage facility.

"Jersey City is cheaper than storage facilities in New York. Have you ever tried storage in Manhattan? It's like you're paying rent for an apartment. And I'm going to continue to be on the road until the end of 1998. But I'm working, which is all I've been wanting for a really long time," he adds.

"I'm not complaining, you know. I'm pinching myself every night. I can't imagine writing something better than this. But I mean, why is all of this happening to me? And if people are expecting this much, will they be mad if I let them down? I don't want to be a flash in the pan. I don't want to lose it all."

# FOURTEEN

**One of the first lessons Matt learned during his introduction** to the Hollywood marketing machine is that it's very hard to keep one's private life private. During the filming of *Good Will Hunting* and throughout the summer he was in Europe filming *Saving Private Ryan*, Damon and Driver had conducted their affair in relative privacy, as far as the public was concerned.

But as journalists saw their body language toward one another during press junkets for *Good Will Hunting*—not to mention the kissing breaks they would share between interviews—word about the romance began to bubble to the surface, and soon both Matt and Minnie were confronted with questions about their relationship.

At first, Matt was dutifully vague.

"Yes, I do have a steady girlfriend. She's great, but I don't like talking about her. We talked about it, and she said don't mention her."

Later, once he was well-established, and he and Minnie were a couple, Matt still avoided getting revealing too much, saying he didn't want to talk about it so as "not to screw it up. She's so British."

Of the two, it seemed as if it was Driver who was more concerned with keeping their romance under wraps, and again, it centered around her concern that her acting in *Good Will Hunting* would somehow be less valid. But over the course of time, Matt slowly began to open up more, even if it was just explaining why he felt reticent to talk about their relationship while promoting the movie.

"I am careful about talking about it because I don't want anything to detract from the work she did in the movie. She's a magnificent actress."

Eventually, Driver herself owned up to the relationship and in talking about it, revealed someone who had felt burned before by knowledge of behind-the-scene romances. Of which she was no stranger, as it happened. Minnie had been briefly linked with her *Circle of Friends* costar Chris O'Donnell and had been openly involved with John Cusack when they were filming *Grosse Point Blank*.

"You know, I can't stand the thought that it may detract from my work," Driver explained. "You know, the thought of people thinking, 'Oh, that's really good because they're in love with each other.' I've been trying to play it down an enormous amount, but there comes a point where you really can't."

To Matt, Driver's work in the film was a separate issue from their romance.

"I fell in love with her," emphasizes Damon. "I don't think either one of us took the characters home with us."

The relationship was serious enough that while on their whirlwind promotional tour for *Good Will Hunting*, Matt took Driver home to meet his mother, family, and friends in Boston.

And going into the holiday season of 1997, Matt was telling his friends that he was madly in love with Minnie and he seemed to be enjoying the simple things with her.

"Our idea of fun, if we ever get a night off, is doing a crossword puzzle in bed before the news."

If there was a drawback, it was his suddenly loaded work schedule, but even that didn't seem to daunt Damon.

"We're both working, so it's difficult. We really have to work at it, but if we want it, we can have it. Maybe it's naive but I really feel that way. I have a lot of work ahead of me this year, but I really want to have that relationship. She's awesome."

Because so much of the publicity generated between October and December, 1997, focused on Matt, there were some who wondered if this wasn't the beginning of the end for Matt and Ben's inseparable friendship. Could Damon's friendship with Affleck remain unaffected by Matt being cast as the Next Big Thing with Ben put in the role of sidekick? The two most unconcerned people seemed to be Matt and Ben. Can his long friendship with Affleck remain unaffected as well?

"We're not competitive," said Affleck. "We've always rooted for each other and I think that's the key to a successful friendship. You can't be too competitive. If there's a part out there and I'm not gonna get it, I'd rather it be Matt than anyone else."

Although Ben wasn't above needling his friend about being the new It boy and teen idol.

"I'm still just standing out there going, 'Hi, I'm Ben. Nice to meet you.' And they just walk on by. But Matt, he's on fire, let me tell you."

The truth was, Ben was doing just fine. Although he wasn't getting the same avalanche of hype heaped on him, he was enjoying a career surge of his own, having been cast in *Armageddon* opposite Bruce Willis.

Nor was Matt the only one in love. As the release date neared for *Good Will Hunting*, Affleck was also in the throes of new love, having begun dating Brad Pitt's ex-fiancée Gwyneth Paltrow.

As the premiere date for *The Rainmaker* neared, Matt became more anxious and more reflective. If *The Rainmaker* bombed, he knew it would dampen the prospects for *Good Will Hunting*. That's just the way the business worked. But if *The Rainmaker* held up with decent reviews and solid box office, then the stage would be set for *Good Will Hunting*.

And none of it was in his hands. After all the talking he had done, after all the interviews, after all the personal appearances, it was now a simple matter of what the critics and movie-goers thought. Which is what it had always been.

"My life, my life with my family, it's all going to be affected by what the press thinks. I do everything in my power to do the best I can, but at this point I have no control over what happens. I'm at the point now where I kind of have to let it go and if nobody buys a ticket to these movies, then that's it for me.

"A lot of my own life and things that affect me personally are going to be decided over the next few weeks, and have nothing to do with me, or anything I can control so it's an anxious time."

It was also a reflective time. Anyone standing on the cusp of fame can't help but peer over the edge and wonder what lies on the rocks below. However, there's no way to know what it will feel like to go off the edge until one actually jumps. But his initial peek at fame hadn't been unpleasant.

"I like it. I don't think I'm addicted to what is involved with it. I really could take it or leave it. So far, I'd have to say I honestly haven't met a single person, I have not walked down the street where someone stopped me and said, 'Oh, you're Matt

Damon.' Not for a movie, not for a magazine cover, not for nothing. Which is normal since not that many people know me for my work, which works fine for me.

"I don't mind if my life changes," Damon says. "The question is, change into *what*? There are a lot of people I see who get celebrity and end up being pretty lonely. They end up raping and pillaging the temptations. They end up standing there in middle age saying, 'What the hell happened?' I would not want to live like that. There's a part of me that wants to have that smaller, manageable, *normal* life."

One way to maintain that normalcy was to keep himself grounded via visits back to his home. And while there, Damon would make it clear that he was the same guy then as he was a year earlier when nobody on the street knew who he was.

Says friend Aaron Stackard: "Whenever he comes through town, he just wants to watch a movie or play video games or go to a bar. The only difference is that he picks up the bill more often."

Staying in touch with his pre-Hollywood roots seemed to be a talisman necessary to ward off the changes being brought by his newfound celebrity. Which, as far as Minnie Driver was concerned, wasn't necessarily such a bad thing because to her, Damon's time in the spotlight was long overdue.

"I know it seems like some finger has come out of the sky and chosen him. He's seen it before. But Matt deserves it. It's right. It's justice. Somehow he got left out of the mix. He knows that being the flavor of the month will be over when the month is over. It's a scary thing. But everybody's lucky to get their shot and I don't think you can find a better actor."

But to Matt, fame and notoriety was a slippery thing

and if one wasn't careful, you could lose your balance and come crashing down.

"It's weird, the celebrity doesn't really mean much yet. I've stayed in touch will all my friends, so it's not like I'm 'returning home.' My friends from high school kid me. They tell me they see my face everywhere. To them its like, 'God, I can't get away from you. You're on the cover of everything.' Their opinion counts so much to me. That won't change, will it?"

Keeping in touch with his childhood friends and family serves the added function of reminding Matt who he is and why he got into acting in the first place. And it clarifies the distinction between the art of acting and the business of acting.

"Ed Burns told me this story when I was doing *Saving Private Ryan* with him. He was at a Yankees game with his girlfriend. And he's buying a hot dog and the hot dog guy goes, 'Hey, Eddie Burns. Love your movies.' And he goes, 'Oh, thank you.' Then the guy goes, 'Listen, *She's the One*, they didn't put it on 800 screens for two weeks. What's up with that?'

"That's what's going on—the guy selling you hot dogs is giving you advice on how many screens to open or platform your movie. It's absolutely a business, and I think business decisions should be made before and after you play the role, but I don't think you should play the role with that in mind or else you're just going to be a lousy actor."

*The Rainmaker* premiered in November 1997. There was a strong *Good Will Hunting* contingent on hand to give Matt moral support, including director Gus Van Sant who spent part of the evening chatting amiably with Matt's dad, Kent. Later, Van Sant would relate a telling comment from the elder Damon.

"Kent said when Matt was little and wanted something, it was watch out! He went after it."

# MATT DAMON

The courtroom drama was met with mixed reviews, typical for a movie based on a Grisham book. However, for the first time, Damon was uniformly singled out for his performance and charisma.

*Sacramento Bee* critic Joe Baltake's effusive praise was typical.

"Coppola's casting is flawless. Damon, a talented young actor on the brink of stardom, gives Rudy just the right blend of innocence, determination, and wariness. He makes a preposterous situation as plausible as it can be. DeVito is a riot as Deck Shifflet, a hardworking opportunist who can't pass a person in the hallway without producing a business card.

"Voight is having a nice second career playing villains, and he's terrific as Drummond, a condescending Goliath being plumped for the courtroom kill by his unlikely opponent. Even Rourke, as the ironic shyster who keeps live sharks in his office, is fun to watch."

Just as important, *The Rainmaker* was performing well at the box office. So the first hurdle had been cleared and it was now official—Matt could "open" a movie, meaning, he could carry a film as leading man. This was no small thing to the studio powers-that-be.

"Matt garnered lots of name recognition for *The Rainmaker*," says Jim Woodin, media coordinator for Edwards Cinema. "People coming to the theater to see the film referred to it as *that Matt Damon picture*. Damon's boy-next-door quality appeals to audiences and he appears very comfortable on the screen."

The publicity and marketing machine had obviously done their job thus far but Matt preferred to concentrate on the communal success of the film, rather than bask in personal glory.

"It's been cool. We all worked hard on the movie, real hard, and made a lot of personal sacrifices, and it feels good that people like it. Hopefully, people will go see it. Yeah, it's tempting to know the box office, but I think in a lot of ways it's dangerous.

"I mean, the reviews were really good for *The Rainmaker* and that felt rewarding 'cause I busted my ass on that movie—moving to Knoxville, bartending, and doing all that stuff to try and get Rudy and he's really different from Will."

And with the two movies coming out so close together, it was particularly important to Damon that the characters be as unique and distinct as possible.

"Roles change per decade, from your twenties to your thirties. I'm a slave to how I look and what I can play so it feels good to have these two characters coming out at around the same time that are so different because it helps me in not getting pigeonholed. However, I don't mind playing young, coming-of-age stories for a while."

Although pleased to have the public and critics finally recognize his work, Damon makes it clear that he doesn't *need* that kind of validation as long as he knows in his heart he's doing the best job he can.

"I'm always pleased with my performances because I know that I couldn't do it any better. I always try my hardest, give it all I've got. If people don't like it, then they don't like it—that's totally up to them. But I'll never have a regret about it.

"*Good Will Hunting* is a lot about that, about not having regrets in life. If it's putting on a lot of weight, if it's going to bartend, or whatever it is, fine if you don't like it. You just do whatever it takes to get to the truth of the character. I don't think there's any length you should not go to do that. That's what we do for a living."

But Damon seems to be acutely intent on keeping it all in perspective.

"I am not deluded into thinking that I know everything. I am the best actor that I can be right now because I have worked as hard as I can. But that just means *only* that I am the best actor I can be. It doesn't mean I am better than anybody. It doesn't mean I am good. It just means I work hard."

For as much as he wanted *The Rainmaker* to do well, Matt had a much deeper personal investment in *Good Will Hunting*. It was one thing for people to not like a film he had merely been an actor-for-hire in. It was another thing altogether to be judged on the film's content as well.

All studios now do audience testing on their films. Many times, it's the results of these surveys that can fuel the all-important buzz on a film. Usually, studios like to keep the results of the surveys a secret, but inevitably the figures leak out.

One of the best known sources of audience-screening information is Harry Knowles, who runs the Internet site, Ain't It Cool News. Knowles has made a cottage industry out of ferreting out information on upcoming films and determining the buzz by encouraging participants to share what they saw with the rest of the cyber world. In the case of *Good Will Hunting*, the buzz was uniformly positive.

More informally, Gus Van Sant experienced a similar response.

"I haven't really had anyone I've shown it to not like the film, which is really unusual for me," laughs the director. "I guess that before, I felt that portraying something out of the mainstream was a powerful way to tell a story. But this time, the story itself was enough."

With *The Rainmaker* released and doing well, Matt braced for the next hurdle, the reviews and public reception to *Good Will Hunting*. But within days of *The*

*Rainmaker*'s release, he began to get his first taste of what it really meant to be a public figure.

"I got off a plane and there were paparazzi there. I said, 'What is going on? Guys, how did you even hear about me?' And they said, 'We wait in the airport for every New York flight and whoever's on it, we take their picture.' I felt better—I'm not being stalked."

But those last vestiges of anonymity were about to dissolve in the juggernaut that would be *Good Will Hunting.*

# FIFTEEN

*Good Will Hunting* had its Los Angeles premiere in December, 1997, at the Bruin Theater in Westwood, the area of L.A. best known as the home of the UCLA Bruins. Gus Van Sant, Robin Williams, Ben, Matt, and Minnie were all in attendance but Damon seemed far more overwhelmed than any of the others, including Ben.

When he stepped out of the limousine and was blinded by the photographers' flashing strobes and disoriented by the mass of humanity calling out his name, Matt literally clung to his agent, Patrick Whitesell.

"It's happening," he yelled breathlessly in Whitesell's ear. "This is it. Oh my God, this is it."

After the movie, everyone moved on to the party, where Damon and Affleck were drowning in a sea of congratulations. Matt's ex-flame Claire Danes was there and ran up to her *Rainmaker* costar and gave him a big hug. "You were wonderful."

In keeping with the movie's South Boston setting, the after-premiere party served clam chowder and Boston cream pie but neither Matt nor Ben ate very much. They were higher than any illicit drug could ever possibly send them.

"People just seem to like the movie and we just feel

like we kind of won the lottery," Ben said, trying to explain the feelings he and Matt were experiencing. "We're really happy we got great people like Robin Williams and Gus Van Sant because how can you go wrong?"

Watching the crowd respond to the movie with laughter and tears was like an out-of-body experience for the two friends.

"It feels like stepping into someone else's life," Affleck said.

Two days later, the three costars attended the New York City premiere of the film. Once again, Matt and Ben were literally mobbed, particularly Damon. Reporters and photographers were screaming his name and jockeying for position to either take his picture or ask him a question for that night's sound bite.

The after-party was held at Manhattan's Redeye Grill and among the many celebrities showing up for the festivities were Rosie Perez, Liv Tyler, Affleck's new love interest Gwyneth Paltrow, longtime buddy Joaquin Phoenix, Peter Bogdanovich, Vince Vaughn, Kathleen Turner and even Little Steven of the Bruce Springsteen band, and Anne Heche, probably best known at that time as Ellen DeGeneres's lover.

Heche was particularly enthusiastic about the work Matt and Ben had done. "How brilliant these guys are!" she gushed. "I'm here to celebrate them."

Damon seemed almost shell-shocked at the outpouring of attention and praise. "I can't put this scene into words because I have nothing to compare it to."

Lawrence Bender did. As the producer on *Pulp Fiction*, he had witnessed the reemergence of John Travolta. But that paled in comparison to the impact Damon would have on the movie industry.

"Normally when this s--- happens in Hollywood, I

say, 'Okay, here we go again.' But Matt has f---ing talent. I mean, who writes a script like this and stars in it? Who, since *Rocky*?"

It was an apt comparison. In the years since Sylvester Stallone broke through with his masterpiece, there had been other actors who had written scripts with parts for themselves. For the most part, the scripts done by the likes of Gary Sinise, Emma Thompson, and Kenneth Branagh were based on well-established material, and produced after the actors had made a bankable name for themselves.

Others, like Ed Burns, had gone the independent route and slowly built a reputation. But to have tackled and conquered the movies from inside the Hollywood system was indeed a *Rocky*-esque feat.

The critics were literally falling all over themselves searching for superlatives.

David Ansen of *Newsweek* said of Matt: "He's currently starring as the underdog attorney in Francis Ford Coppola's *The Rainmaker* . . . but *Good Will Hunting* is the movie that makes Damon's case—he's sensationally convincing and appealing as this whiz kid, a fascinating mixture of aggression, sweetness, hurt, and intellectual bravado."

"We've got a winner in *Good Will Hunting*," opined Robert Denerstein. "The glow goes well beyond a radiant performance by Matt Damon as a misunderstood, rebellious genius. Intimate, heartfelt, and wickedly funny, it's a movie whose impact lingers.

"Damon is sensational. Even in quiet moments, torment seems to roil under his skin. He turns every gesture of defiance and denial into a revelation. His acting is earthy, audacious, and intelligent."

*USA Today*'s reviewer, Mike Clark, was more restrained but no less impressed.

"Yet the headline story from this slice of honestly earned sentiment is Matt Damon, who delivers the year's No. 1 breakthrough performance directly atop his agreeable high-profile turn in John Grisham's *The Rainmaker*—both after a career of nearly a decade's duration.

"Damon convincingly matches Williams recrimination for recrimination in this portrayal of mutual tough love, even with the latter giving what may be the best performance of his career."

"Damon has been on the rise, earning good notices in . . . the lead role of a novice attorney in the recently released John Grisham's *The Rainmaker*. But it is *Will Hunting* who will make him a major star," offered Jack Matthews of *Newsday*.

"In fact, you may have to go back to Jack Nicholson's Bobby Dupea in *Five Easy Pieces* for a similarly blessed marriage of star to role, and Damon's performance is no less magnetic. He has a commanding presence on screen, mixing boyish good looks with a voice fermented in oak, and he has the ability to seem simultaneously dangerous and sympathetic.

"In the end, *Good Will Hunting* is less a great movie than a great opportunity. For Matt Damon, it's A Star is Born."

And it wasn't only America smitten with Damon's turn in the film. Quentin Curtis from London's *The Daily Telegraph*, believed Matt's potential as a Hollywood star was unlimited.

"Damon is very good—potentially even great. With his fresh face, but firm drawl and stocky frame, he pulls off a rare double act: he is sensitive at the same time as solid, sweet as well as macho—both an aesthete and a hearty. His appeal could be unlimited. The toothy features are of a less streamlined Tom Cruise, as if the cockiness had been flattened away."

But Curtis also sounds a mild warning bell about the celebrity marketing machine that helped promote Matt and the film.

"Knowing so much about Damon interferes with his art. Damon deserves all the praise he's receiving—but that doesn't mean it's a help to him or us."

It was obvious the critics were won over. Now all Matt could do was sit back and see if the public felt the same.

*Good Will Hunting* opened December 5 in selected cities. Even though the movie opened on only seven screens, it pulled in an enormous per-screen average of $37,143, grossing $260,000. It was then that Miramax knew for sure it had a winner on its hands. The ink on the first box office tally was barely dry before the Miramax publicity brain trust were busy at work planning the next phase in the life of *Good Will Hunting*—planning and mounting an Oscar campaign.

With the one-two punch of *Good Will Hunting* and *The Rainmaker* both making a noise at the box office, Matt Damon went from being Hollywood's Next Big Thing to the reigning It boy. He had proven through two very different films that he was more than just hype—that he had the talent and charisma to back it up. He was the real thing—a true movie star who also happened to be a good actor.

The reason critics and entertainment writers most often compared Damon to Matthew McConaughey as opposed to other young actors such as Edward Norton or Ethan Hawke was twofold. The most obvious was the fact they were both thrust into the public eye via a John Grisham film, each playing idealistic young lawyers who win cases believed to be a lost cause. And both had been hailed by *Time* Magazine as "Hollywood's Newest Golden Boy"—McConaughey on July 29, 1996, and Damon on December 1, 1997

The other reason was more a matter of personality. Many of the younger actors exuded a sullen, almost adolescent demeanor. They were openly contemptuous of the publicity process and uncommunicative with journalists during interviews and press junkets.

But Damon and McConaughey were throwbacks to a different kind of movie actor. They were gregarious and charming and polite and willing to put themselves out to help promote the movie. They understood the business side of the entertainment business and participated in it without resentment, without it affecting their joy of acting.

"It's important never to be defined by the publicity spin, by the spin doctors," Matt says. "At the end of the day, they are like two different jobs, acting and publicity. Publicity is a full-time gig and I can see why it causes consternation for some people. Because when it goes away, people are constantly left screaming, 'Where did it go? Why did it happen?' "

The fact that Damon and McConaughey are friends made the comparison of the two that much more amusing to Matt. But Matt was leery of being compared to anyone, of being the next whomever. He simply wanted to be first Matt Damon.

"I won't be Matthew McConaughey. I'm not as good-looking as him. And I'm certainly not going to be anyone's sex symbol."

Try telling that to the women flocking to see his movies. However, Damon was one of those actors who women can see themselves cuddling and men can imagine sharing a beer with—an image that was immeasurably reinforced by his performance in *Good Will Hunting*.

Theater-chain owner Bob Laemmle agrees. "Damon's popularity is solid. It's very simple: he makes good choices and he's been in good films. And in *Good Will Hunting* audiences have found a connection with the dialogue—it's superb."

"I like to call Matt Damon a Tom Cruise-in-waiting," says Nina Malkin, deputy editor of *Teen* magazine, which has a circulation of 1.8 million readers. "Matt is a bridge baby—somebody who appeals to the teenage audience and also the twentysomethings.

"For our older readers, those fifteen and sixteen, he's going to be a very main attraction. To our younger readers, he's already a grown-up!"

Miramax cochairman, Harvey Weinstein thought it was important not to only see Damon as a business asset and commodity.

"With all the well-deserved praise that's been heaped on Matt in the past four months, it's difficult to say something about his enormous talent as a writer and actor that hasn't been said already.

"What I can add, though, is that Matt is a wonderful human being. He is exceptionally bright, honest, and levelheaded and has both feet planted firmly on the ground, which is a hard thing to do in this business.

"I couldn't be happier for him, for everything that he has achieved."

The conventional wisdom in Hollywood was that *Good Will Hunting* was a shoo-in for several Golden Globe and Oscar nominations, especially with Miramax's marketing muscle behind it.

On December 17, Matt Damon was nominated for a Blockbuster Award as favorite actor. The award was essentially a public popularity poll sponsored by the giant video rental company. Although Damon would eventually lose out to the other hot actor of the moment, *Titanic* star and *uber* teen-idol, Leonardo DiCaprio, it was indicative of just how much the public had embraced Matt.

While magazine covers and newspaper interviews can make the public aware of an actor, it's no guarantee the audience will respond on a gut level. But they had to Matt and the Blockbuster nomination showed he now had an audience who would go see a movie simply to see him.

A day later, on December 18, the Hollywood Foreign Press announced the nominations for the Golden Globes. It was all Miramax had hoped for and more. Matt was nominated for Best Actor, he and Ben were nominated for Best Screenplay, and *Good Will Hunting* snagged a Best Picture nomination.

It was almost more than Matt could compute and it took a conscious effort to put it all in perspective. While Damon understood the importance of awards, as always, he was more concerned with what the awards buzz meant to his acting. And so far, it was only positive. For the first time in his career, he was put in the position of having "name" directors seeking him out

"I can't believe I'm in a position where I have to turn down work. This has never happened. The funny thing is," he says, "that as soon as you get big, the studios send you these scripts that they've been trying to get made for twenty years, that were originally written for Dustin Hoffman. They've been sitting on the shelf. You get their old standbys."

One film Matt had been erroneously attached to was *To Live On*, Ang Lee's next project.

"I was never attached to that film," Damon clarifies.

"I read that in *Variety* and couldn't believe that happened. Literally, there was no 'I'm doing this movie and here's a contract.' It wasn't like that. Ang said, 'I really want to work with you' and I really wanted to work with Ang and so everybody got excited. Producer James Shamus said I might do *To Live On*, so their movie started getting attention. It was bizarre."

But the best part of having some clout and "juice" is that the studios were more willing to indulge an actor like Damon to do whatever research he felt necessary prior to working on a film.

"I want to be in a position where I can go wherever the character I'm researching is supposed to be from. The nice thing is that I'm in a position now where they're actually paying me to do it. I mean, they're putting me up during the time I research, which is what I used to have to do out of pocket like for *Courage Under Fire* and *The Rainmaker*."

The research Damon had most recently delved into was for his next movie, *Rounders*, which takes place in the world of Manhattan's questionably legal poker clubs and for which Damon was paid $600,000. In the film, directed by John Dahl, Damon plays a cardshark who leaves behind gambling to attend law school in hopes of building a legitimate life with his girlfriend, played by actress Gretchen Mol. But Matt's character gets sidetracked when one of his friends, played by Edward Norton, who has recently been released from jail, desperately needs help paying off a loanshark.

John Malkovich plays a local Russian who runs the biggest, and most dangerous, poker game in town. Also in the cast is John Turturro as Damon's gambling mentor and Martin Landau as his law school professor.

The movie, written by Brian Koppelman and David Levien, was based on Koppelman's own experiences of playing poker in college. "Now that I've sold the screenplay," jokes Brian, "I can honestly tell my mother I've made money playing poker."

Even before filming was complete, there was a new buzz about Matt—that *Rounders*, another Miramax film, would elevate him from stardom to Leonardo DiCaprio-esque super-stardom.

When Damon and Norton started going to the underground clubs in order to get a feel for that world and to learn how to play, nobody knew who these two fresh-faced young men were. And in keeping with club etiquette, as it were, only first names are used. As it turned out, both Matt and Ed were quick studies and were soon playing in the high-stakes games, betting thousands of dollars on single hands. And winning.

Apparently, being shown up by a couple of amateurs, pretty boys from Hollywood no less, did not sit well with many of the men who consider themselves professional gamblers. And when Matt and Ed showed up at the World Series of Poker, held at Binion's Horseshoe Hotel and Casino in Las Vegas, there was a bounty on their heads, so to speak. Whoever knocked them out of the competition would earn a cash bonus.

The tournament proved that neither Damon nor Norton should give up their day jobs anytime soon. Both were knocked out in the early rounds. Although, they are still a terror on the Hollywood circuit. The pair won over $1,200 from Harvey and Bob Weinstein in a friendly game played during the filming of *Rounders*.

Although to the rest of the movie world, it may have seemed as if Matt had suddenly appeared over the last three months out of cinema nowhere, to Damon it had been a long time in coming. And now with the benefit of hindsight, Matt was glad that his time had come later as opposed to sooner.

"A few years ago, I would have told you that it should have happened for me then. But I'm glad it happened this way. It does give me more perspective. I'd like to think that, anyway. I've walked down the red carpet for *School Ties*, *Geronimo*, and *Courage Under Fire* with everyone going, 'Matt! Matt! Over here!' and they're taking pictures. And the first two movies bombed. It was a real lesson in humility. That stuff is all so f---ing fleeting, you know."

What made his current situation that much more satisfying was that it included Ben.

"I can't even wrap my brain around the idea that not only is it happening, but it's happening for me and Ben both. It's great. It's so much better that celebrity happened to both of us at the same time. It makes it more special. To look over and see it happening to your best friend is pretty cool.

"It's so much better than doing it alone. And it's easier for me to get perspective on what's happening to me because I take a look at what's happening to Ben. I'm able to see it as an outsider."

Robin Williams, for one, thought Damon had the perfect perspective. "Matt makes fun of himself. He's going to do great."

One of the more endearing qualities about Matt was his ability to let the little kid in him shine through. He wasn't concerned with maintaining a hip or I'm-too-cool-for-this or blasé attitude about the fun it was to suddenly be famous and a celebrity.

"The best part of this is all the free stuff!" he laughs, delighted. "Everywhere. At the hotels, you don't have to pay for your minibar. I'm going to pig out on the minibar while I can—that stuff's pretty expensive. Those cashews are like four bucks. But I eat them, and order overpriced room-service food that I would never pay for myself.

"And I got a free suit. I went to Calvin Klein. They tried all these things on me and said I looked very *fash*. They promised me that I'll look *fash*."

His attitude to enjoy the perks without taking himself too seriously bode well against Matt ever alienating his friends and family by starting to believe his own press releases.

"I can't fathom that happening," he says firmly. "It takes a concentrated effort and it's a matter of choice. The temptation is to disregard reality and live in a world where you're the king and everyone else is a subject. A lot of people do that. But that would be horrible. The isolation would be so profound. And that's reserved for Elvis. I just want to be able to laugh at myself and buy eggs at the store and not live a weird life.

"Fame will f--- you if you're not ready for it and it will f--- you if you're not grounded. I've got a great family and I'm surrounded by people I love and trust who will not hesitate to knock me down if they see me getting arrogant.

"Besides, I don't feel any different. I still work fifteen hours a day."

Although Affleck says he could understand why some actors turn into jerks once their star rises.

"I do see how it happens that actors become monsters. One thing is the enormous number of actors who get treated badly all the time. They're herded through great rooms and treated like meat. They do extra work and are made to feel insignificant.

"We've all had that time when nobody gave a crap about you, nobody cared to be nice to you. There's a side of the business that likes to treat actors who aren't stars badly. 'We have to kiss this guy's butt, but we can treat you poorly and there's nothing you can do about it.' That kind of resentment builds up.

"Also, the rewards of stardom are so out of whack. In general, actors are pretty self-centered people to begin with. To make matters worse, the yes-men around them create the illusion that the star is far more important than he is. It creates a great ego and once you've created that ego, to accept anything less than royal treatment is a blow to that ego."

Affleck was also struck by how quickly fortunes can change in Hollywood.

"You know, it wasn't that long ago that Matt and I would be sitting home and we'd be watching *Oprah*, going like, 'These guys aren't that good. We're better than these guys.' And then all of a sudden, you're kind of out there and it's like, a very surreal, weird sort of transition when you're the one sitting in front of the audience."

Unlike many young actors who go off the deep end when suddenly awash in ridiculous amounts of money—it was Robin Williams who once cracked, "Cocaine is God's way of telling you you're making too much money"—Damon's lifestyle had hardly changed at all, despite the large paychecks he was now earning. In fact, the money seemed almost unreal.

"I saved my money. I helped my mom get a house and my brother's college is taken care of. *Saving Private Ryan* was his college."

But Matt was well aware that sudden money can be overwhelming and seem like a giant crapshoot.

"One guy wins the lottery and goes through all the money and then somebody else wins," he notes. "We've seen people burn through money and it *is* like winning the lottery, but only better because I've also learned a lot."

And one of the things he learned was that he didn't want to become one of those celebrities who suddenly think they are more than what they really are—actors. Not only was Damon sought after by reporters and fans, but he was now being deluged by charities to attach his name to their various causes.

"Because somebody is on a television show or in a movie, does that qualify them to talk about an important issue?" he wondered. "I have no problem with people who walk it like they talk it, but very few people do.

"It's easy when everyone's paying attention to you to say, 'Well, here's a cause.' But very few actors are moving out of their houses or getting out of their Range Rovers to pick up their fellow man. Those few who do are the real thing and they usually don't talk about it.

"Look, I totally believe you should do things to better the world, but oftentimes there's so much bulls--- that just rings so hollow it kind of mucks up the waters. I think that some actors are more interested in having people think they want to help people than in actually helping them."

If there was a blip on Matt's happiness screen at all, it involved Ben. While basking in the warmth of glory generated by *Good Will Hunting*, Damon couldn't help but feel a sense of regret that Affleck wasn't receiving the same amount of attention he was. Without Ben, there would have been no *Good Will Hunting*.

"The biggest sadness I have is that I look at my role in *Good Will Hunting* and I think that Ben could have easily have played it. I think he let me do it because literally, he's my best friend in the world and he's that selfless," Matt once said in an interview, his voice briefly choking up.

But he quickly regained his composure and joked: "But hey, don't feel bad for Ben. He's saving the world. Didn't anyone tell you there's an asteroid the size of Texas headed toward the earth? And if it weren't for Ben and Bruce Willis, God knows what would happen."

# SIXTEEN

**The New Year began where 1997 had left off—with Matt** still at the eye of a media hurricane. Miramax was going full speed in their campaign to secure Matt and Ben a Best Original Screenplay nomination and were hoping to sneak in a Best Picture nod as well. They were also waging a separate campaign for Robin Williams, with ads appearing in the entertainment dailies asking Academy members to consider his for a Best Supporting Actor nomination.

So instead of a media blitz centering around Matt himself, now it was Damon, Affleck, and Williams who seemed to be on every talk show and entertainment news magazine. On one such appearance, *The Oprah Winfrey Show*, Matt revealed that contrary to public opinion, he and Minnie Driver were no longer a romantic item.

"Well, I'm single," he answered in response to a question from Winfrey. "I was with Minnie for a while, but we're not really romantically involved anymore. We're just really good friends and I love her dearly.

"I care a lot about her. We care about each other a lot. It was just, we decided it wasn't meant to be. And if it's not meant to be, then it's not meant to be."

The only problem, according to subsequent reports,

was that apparently Damon hadn't bothered to tell Driver yet before announcing their breakup on national television. She was said to not be amused. Within days of the *Oprah* revelation, the tabloids were crawling all over the breakup, trying to ferret out who had broken up with whom and why.

According to the *National Enquirer*, Minnie was allegedly the one to break it off with Matt. She was tired of Matt always being around so she dumped him in front of Steven Spielberg at a dinner party and that Spielberg had to console Matt. To even the most fervent Driver supporter, the story sounded fantastical.

A slightly less outlandish-sounding version was that Minnie or some of her people were a little too anxious to capitalize on her relationship with Matt. According to friends of Damon, somebody kept tipping off the celebrity photographers about where Matt and Minnie would be going so there would be a pack of paparazzi wherever and whenever they went out, even if the destination had been a last-minute decision.

What gave the story some credence was that well-known celebrity gossip *meister* Liz Smith reported in one of her columns how Driver's publicist had called her complaining because Smith had failed to mention Driver's appearance at some event she attended with Matt, with the flack wanting it pointed out that Driver was there as Damon's girlfriend.

The fact is, many, many actors become involved on films only to have the romance flicker out once the movie is over and the couple is thrust back into the reality of daily living. Filming on location is in many ways like taking a real-life trip to *Fantasy Island*. Actors are thrust into a pretend existence and paired up with other attractive actors and it's easy to believe you're in love. Whatever the underlying causes of their breakup, the aftermath was not an amicable one, indicating that one side had not wanted the relationship to be over. And later events would certainly indicate it was Matt's decision to end the affair.

When asked during an online chat if he still talked to Minnie, Damon answered obliquely.

"I still talk to Skylar. No bad blood there at all . . . "

Damon's breakup with Driver, his alleged brief affair with Courtney Love, and the fact that he had been romantically linked with Claire Danes during the filming of *The Rainmaker* was giving Matt a bit of a reputation as a ladies' man. Although when Oprah Winfrey asked Matt if it was easy to fall for a leading lady, he seemed flustered.

"I don't know," he claimed. "I haven't done that much to know."

However, Matt met the woman who would next steal his heart the old-fashioned way—he was set up by friends. By early 1998, Ben Affleck was openly involved with Gwyneth Paltrow and one of her best friends was actress Winona Ryder. So it was through Ben and Gwyneth that Matt met Winona. And it wasn't long before Damon found himself once again falling in love.

At the time they began dating, Ryder was just ending a self-imposed year's hiatus. During that time she rented an apartment near her parents in San Francisco and was hanging with her childhood friends. When contacted by Liz Smith, though, the usually candid Winona admitted she was "seriously dating" Matt Damon.

According to Smith: "Winona says stories of her dating everyone from David Duchovny were untrue. 'I had like two dates in the last year and they weren't with anyone famous. If I was getting all the action they say, I would die. You know, a date doesn't mean you kiss or sleep with the person either.'

"Of Damon and Winona, an observer says, 'Yes, he's in love. But he's twenty-eight. So of course he is.' "

On January 19, 1998, the Golden Globe Awards were presented at the Beverly Hilton Hotel. Although the sponsoring Hollywood Foreign Press Club only consisted of around 100 members, the Golden Globes had taken on ever-increasing importance to studio marketing departments, who had floated the perception that the Globes were a precursor of the Oscars—even though there was no overlap in the memberships and it was well-believed throughout Hollywood that it was more than possible to sway the Foreign Press voting if enough lunches were bought and enough freebies given away.

Because the Golden Globes also honor television, it sometimes seems as if every star in Hollywood attends the event, and 1998 was no exception. Matt and Ben arrived looking wide- and glassy-eyed. Their exuberance was a refreshing change from the often-staid countenances of more established stars. It was obvious they were truly just happy to have been invited to the party.

When their names were announced as winners of the Best Screenplay award, their delight was contagious. Backstage, the met an applauding press corps and tried to put their feelings into coherent words. But even through their happiness, they remained humble.

"We're trying to let it soak in," said Affleck, who tends to often talk more than Matt when the two are together, with Damon happily deferring to his friend. "We know so many writers whose work we admire and whose work we respect, it's hard not to feel like an impostor—to feel like the Milli Vanilli of screenwriting."

Ben also admitted that he felt intimidated now being included with people who just a year ago were distant idols.

"It's like being in a room full of your heroes. You

look out there and think, What on earth are we doing here? Here are all these brilliant people—it's totally overwhelming. Jim Carrey gave us a thumbs-up which was pretty cool."

When asked the obligatory *where are you going to put your award* question, Damon laughed.

"I don't have a home, so I'll probably just carry it with me. My toothbrush and my Golden Globe."

Matt addressed the question about what they owed Miramax.

"I think we'll have to work for Harvey Weinstein for the next thirty or forty years," he joked, then added on a more serious note, "at the end of the day, we just wanted to make something that we liked. We weren't really making it for the purpose of mass consumption. We're so happy everybody wants to see it. It's a gratifying feeling.

"But now, everyone is saying, 'Well, *when's your next movie?*'"

"And we're like, 'What?'" says Ben. "*Isn't one enough?*"

The nominations for the Academy Awards are announced in Los Angeles at the pre-dawn hour of 5:30 A.M. so they can be broadcast live during the morning talk shows on the East Coast. The West Coast press are not terribly pleased at having to get up in the middle of the night to accommodate network desires and often show up looking half asleep. But the studio and personal publicists on hand tend to be bouncing off the walls in anticipation.

Miramax wasn't disappointed. Just as in the Golden Globes, they pulled off the main nominations they had been seeking, Best Actor for Damon, Best Supporting Actor for Robin Williams, Best Original Screenplay for

Damon and Affleck and the big one, Best Picture.

From the moment the nominations were announced, Matt and Ben were considered the favorites to win the Oscar for their screenplay. In part because it indeed held together very well as a movie but also because of the fairy-tale nature of their efforts to get the movie made. Hollywood still loves an underdog. It was *Rocky* revisited.

To Damon, it was too much to even hope for. "Oh, boy. No, man, it's too much. Definitely too much. I can't even comprehend this."

In a bit of dramatic irony, Matt Damon and Minnie Driver were named the Male and Female Stars of Tomorrow and the ceremony was held at the ShoWest convention on March 12 in Las Vegas. From all accounts, the tension was palpable when both Driver and Damon shared the stage during the presentation, with the two standing on opposite sides of the stage.

Making matters worse was that Damon was clearly not feeling well. It was later reported he was recovering from a case of food poisoning. The previous evening, he had eaten dinner at a Thai restaurant in Los Angeles, then a few hours later went to a local ER for treatment. He was released the following morning—and immediately caught a plane to Las Vegas. He returned to L.A. immediately after, into the waiting arms of Winona Ryder.

Although the weeks leading up to the Academy Awards were as exciting as Matt imagined they would be, they were not without controversy. The first was some sniping being done in the media over the Academy's failure to nominate Leonardo DiCaprio in the Best Actor category. Of the five actors nominated— Robert Duvall, Jack Nicholson, Peter Fonda, Dustin Hoffman, and Matt Damon—it was Damon who was singled out as the one who had "replaced" DiCaprio in the category. Although in fact, nobody knew who had actually been the fifth leading vote-getter.

But there were those who felt that the lead actor in the movie poised to become the most financially successful film in the history of the movies should not have been overlooked. Especially when that actor was on the verge of becoming the next Tom Cruise in terms of international popularity. Not that his popularity or *Titanic's* box office should have influenced the opinion of DiCaprio's performance, but in Hollywood it does.

"A lot of us are having second thoughts about Leonardo," admitted one member of the Academy of Motion Picture Arts and Sciences. "He's a very good performer and he is the star of what's about to become the biggest picture of all time. Perhaps we goofed."

*Titanic* producer Jon Landau called the omission unfortunate but added that, "Leo is going to be a big star for years to come."

The more damaging rumor concerned the authorship of Matt and Ben's script. Shortly after the nomination was announced, a potentially damaging whispering campaign began, and rumors began swirling that the *Good Will Hunting* script did not qualify for the Oscar.

"This has been going on for months," said Tony Angellotti, a spokesman for Miramax Films. "The calls are coming in anonymously. Who's got the most to gain?" he wondered.

One rumor claimed Damon and Affleck had bought the script from someone else. Another insinuated the screenplay had actually been written by veteran film writer William Goldman and the other was that Matt had initially written the story at Harvard as a one-act play.

Of all the insinuations, the last one was potentially

the most troublesome as far as the Academy was concerned and could have jeopardized the best original screenplay nomination if it was proven the story had been performed or published previously.

Miramax moved quickly to clear the air. First, what was bought was the title from a friend of Damon's in Boston. Goldman did indeed meet with Matt and Ben when the project was still at Castle Rock but never wrote a word.

"You know," says a testy Affleck, "Matt and I wrote the script, beginning to end. We sat down with William Goldman, before the *Forget Paris* premiere which we were all attending. Goldman chatted about his movies. We ran into him two months later in Los Angeles and he mistook Matt for his driver."

Matt adds: "Here is the simple fact. I have the handwritten various drafts beginning to end at home.

"People are fighting like mad over credit for various screenplays," he says, referring to claims of plagiarism against the screenwriters of *Amistad* and *Wag the Dog*. "Why wouldn't they come forward and arbitrate?"

"We wrote it," Ben says with finality. "That's all. But I take it as a backhanded compliment that people are so incredulous."

Damon also vehemently denies the story he wrote at Harvard was ever performed as a play.

Bruce Davis, executive director of the Academy of Motion Picture Arts and Sciences, said the writers' branch executive committee had checked into the script's history and found no problems. Otherwise, it would have been moved into the other screenwriting category for "material previously produced or published"—a category it was considered a foregone conclusion that the writers of *L.A. Confidential* would win.

The week prior to the Oscars are full of parties and

events, and although Matt seemed to be having the time of his life, it was a painful time for Driver. First a London newspaper, *The Sun*, broke the story that Minnie and Jack Nicholson had once had a one-night affair years before. According to the paper, Minnie met Jack at a party and after talking for a while, she left with him for his hotel where Minnie supposedly told a friend they "made love all night."

Neither Driver nor Nicholson, Hollywood's still-reigning ladies' man, would comment on the report, although it was reported that Oscar officials went to great logistical lengths to keep Minnie and Jack as far away from each other as possible.

And according to one columnist, Minnie was also doing everything she could to avoid running into Matt. "Their's was a bitter split. At least, she's bitter. Minnie and her parents walked out of the British Academy Awards ceremony on Saturday after they spotted Matt. And though invited, Driver didn't show up at all for Miramax's pre-Oscar bash on Sunday, which was said to be the most fabulous, fun pre-Oscar event. I guess it was a good thing Minnie avoided that party. Matt showed up with Winona Ryder, looking smitten and telling pals he was *madly in love* with her."

Driver missed one hell of a party. At the pre-Oscar bash, Robin Williams teased Harvey Weinstein, known for not paying actors very much, about the grosses for *Good Will Hunting*. In exchange for taking a small upfront salary, far below his normal quote, Williams had been given 15% of the film's *gross*. And as of March 1998, *Good Will Hunting* had taken in more than $115 million domestically alone, with a worldwide projection of $300 million. To put that in perspective, *Pulp Fiction* earned "only" $100 million worldwide for Miramax. Looked at in another way, it meant Robin stood to earn upwards of $45 million for his participation in the film.

Ben got into the act by climbing on a stage and pretending to be Weinstein at the contract signing. Matt had the crowd, which included Madonna, laughing hysterically when he appeared in drag during a skit with Ben parodying the British costume drama, *Mrs. Brown*.

Returning the joke, Dame Judy Dench and Helena Bonham Carter appeared as hard hats from *Good Will Hunting* while Lawrence Bender played the Pam Grier role from *Jackie Brown*.

Whatever happened at the Oscars, Matt felt as if he and Ben were already the big winners just by dint of being allowed to join the Hollywood inner-circle club.

Monday, March 23, was a typical Southern California spring day. Blue sky with an occasional fluffy white cloud floating by. Both Damon's and Affleck's moms were in town, having been asked by their sons to be their official Oscar dates. The actors girlfriends, Gwyneth Paltrow and Winona Ryder, would meet up with Ben and Matt after the televised ceremony so they could make the round of parties together.

As anyone with access to a television or newspaper knew, it was destined to be the year of *Titanic* and most industry analysts and experts expected the film to come close to tying the record of Oscar wins set by *Ben Hur*, with an outside shot at breaking the record.

But there were some categories that were *Titanic*-light: Best Original Screenplay, Best Actor, and Best Supporting Actor. Matt says he was thrilled beyond words when Robin Williams won the Best Supporting Oscar and was touched to the point of tears at Williams's acceptance speech, which singled out Matt and Ben's script.

Damon realized Jack Nicholson was the odds-on

favorite to win the Best Actor award, but so many people were predicting he and Ben would walk away with the screenwriting award that it seemed the Oscar was theirs to lose. So when it was time for the writing categories to be awarded, he and Ben suddenly felt pressure—until they heard their names announced.

Matt and Ben literally sprang out of their seats, like teammates who've just won the World Series on an extra-inning home run. Once up at the podium, Ben did most of the talking.

"I just said to Matt, 'Losing would suck and winning would be really scary.' And it's really, really scary, you know? We're just two young guys who were fortunate enough to be involved with a lot of great people upon whom—it's incumbent on us—there's no way we're doing this in less than twenty seconds—upon whom it's incumbent of us to thank. Harvey Weinstein who believed in us and made this movie. Gus Van Sant for brilliant direction and Robin Williams who delivered such great lines and Minnie Driver."

"Whoever we forgot," Damon said, raising the Oscar above his head, "we love you and thank you very much."

As it happened, they *had* forgotten to thank one very important person—director Kevin Smith, who had personally delivered the *Good Will Hunting* script to Harvey Weinstein.

Two days after the Awards, Affleck posted a *mea culpa* on an Internet message board apologizing for forgetting to thank the fellow that made it all possible way back when.

"Thank you Kevin for making this dream a reality. Look for a piece in the trades to follow.

"Thank you Kevin . . . I figure if I write it a billion times on the board it'll make up for the billion viewers who missed it."

Backstage at the Oscars, Matt and Ben were once again greeted by applause in every media room they entered. It took an obvious conscious effort for them to concentrate on the questions being asked, such as whether or not they planned to write any more movies together.

"Not only do we plan on writing more, we're contracted to do it. So we have to. We have a contract to write three more for less money than the first one sold for, so they were no dummies. They took a risk and it paid off, but we really like it.

"But we're not really writers in the sense that we don't want to be producers who write for other people. There is no point in that for us. That is not our passion. We would rather act. We really just write stuff we would like to act in."

About their ability to work together and stay friends:

"The secret to working together is to abuse each other. If you can't be honest with the guy, you work with him apropos of the point because we don't pull any punches when we critique each other."

And, knowing how critical Matt's mom had been in the past about her son's celebrity, about how their mothers were holding up.

"It was really great to have our moms here and have them see all this stuff. My mom told me just to enjoy the moment. She's considering the Oscar her grandson and she's holding it for ransom until she gets her real one."

When Damon was asked which Oscar he wanted more, the writing or the acting, he stared at the journalist incredulously.

"Are you kidding me? I've never even been here before. I didn't care."

"He just wanted a job, sir," Ben added.

The Miramax Oscar Night party was held at the

Beverly Hills Hotel's Polo Lounge. The previous year the fire marshal had closed down the studio's party because it was so packed with celebrities, so the 1998 version was much more intimate. At least by comparison. Minnie Driver did show up for this soiree but stayed on the opposite end of the room from Damon. Ben, however, made it a point to come up and give her a bear hug. But then again, as someone pointed out, Affleck gave *everyone* in the room a giant bear hug.

"This is so beyond anything we could have wanted," he later said. "Anyone who says they're going to win one of these is either arrogant or an asshole. Or both."

# SEVENTEEN

In April, 1998 *Premiere* ranked Damon the eighty-eighth most powerful person in the magazine's annual *100 Most Powerful* people in Hollywood feature—ahead of Sylvester Stallone in the ninety-eighth position and Demi Moore, who came in at ninety-two. Entertainment columns now regularly followed his comings and goings, especially as it pertained to his romance with Winona Ryder. The couple seemed to be everywhere—at the Dead Man Walking concert, hosted by Susan Sarandon and Tim Robbins and benefiting the victims of crime, jogging at a park near Ryder's home on Saturday mornings and going to the movies in L.A.'s Beverly Center.

Despite the attention and notoriety winning the Oscar had engendered, Matt remained as thoughtful and low-key as ever. He turned down an offer to be the next Calvin Klein underwear poster boy, consistent with his expressed lack of interest in becoming Hollywood's next sex symbol. He wanted to be known as the next great Hollywood actor. And with that in mind, he carefully weighed each job offer for how it would expand him creatively, not how much money it would put into his bank account.

It would have probably been a safer career move to line up a series of big-budget, mainstream, *safe* films to follow-up his *Good Will Hunting* triumph. But Damon has definite thoughts about risk-taking.

"Nobody goes through a career without setbacks and when it happens, it will give me a chance to become a better actor."

But the first project he worked on post-Oscar was largely to repay a debt of gratitude. Both he and Ben were starring in Kevin Smith's next film, a sharp-toothed, irreverent comedy called *Dogma*.

In the film, Affleck and Damon play the angels, Bartleby and Loki, who have been thrown out of heaven. They were banished after Loki, who had been God's avenging angel for many years, is convinced by his friend Bartleby that killing in God's name was not a good thing—this while relaxing after killing all the first-born sons of Egypt.

Realizing Bartleby is right, Loki throws down his flaming sword and quits. However, God tells him he's fired and banishes both angels to Wisconsin for eternity.

Eons later, Bartelby and Loki hear that a local priest has arranged a special day of forgiveness. Anyone walking into the church will have their sins forgiven. The two angels realize this is their chance for redemption and to get back to heaven—a prospect that not everyone in heaven wants to see happen.

*Dogma* began filming in March in Pittsburg, Pennsylvania. When shooting a scene near a bus station in McKeesport, Pennsylvania, the sight of Matt and Ben together caused a major traffic jam—which pleased director Smith to no end, although Damon warned, "Hopefully we won't wear out our welcome before *Dogma* opens."

The movie, scheduled for an August, 1998, release, also stars Dwight Ewell, Linda Fiorentino, Salma Hayek, Jason Lee, Alan Rickman, Chris Rock as Rufus, the for-

# MATT DAMON

gotten thirteenth apostle and, in a rather unconventional casting choice, Alanis Morrisette playing God.

"I'm very pleased that Kevin has given me this opportunity and I hope that people will like my acting as much as they like my music," says the jagged little singer. "Working with movie people has made me want to be in the movies."

The mood on the set was light, with Smith frequently exchanging banter with his two stars. Once during an online interview with an Australian magazine, Damon cracked, "I work for a slave-driving, no-compliment giving, line-reading motherf---er."

To which Smith replied, "Yeah? Well, I work with gay poster boys."

The last jab may have been a reference to an unsubstantiated rumor swirling on the Internet that Damon was a closet homosexual. It's almost a coming-of-career right of passage for any young, handsome actor to face rumors that he's gay. And in some cases, it's true. In most others, it's not. Some of the speculation may have started after *Interview* magazine published pictures of Matt and Ben looking as if they were about to passionately embrace.

And Damon's next film role no doubt furthered speculation among those wishing it were so. In *The Talented Mr. Ripley*, Matt plays a charming bisexual con man, who is driven to murder. Directed by Oscar-winning Anthony Minghella, (*The English Patient*) and based on Patricia Highsmith's novel, the role was originally offered to Tom Cruise, who turned it down. Damon did not have to be asked twice.

"It's the role of a lifetime," he says.

And proving that Hollywood is indeed a very small town, Damon's costar is none other than his best buddy's girlfriend, Gwyneth Paltrow.

Set in the 1950s and scheduled to begin production in Italy in May 1998, the film tells the story of an opportunistic young man hired by the father of a playboy to coax the man's prodigal son home from Italy. But in doing so, Damon's character yearns to live the life of the son himself.

"The character is fascinating," Damon explains. "Ripley goes and falls in love with this man and his life—to the point where he wants to be in his skin. And becomes a sociopathic killer. It's certainly the most unconventional in terms of movies I've ever done. As Anthony says, he's going to be accused of making another big art-house movie."

As always, Damon researched the character extensively in order to bring Ripley to life.

"I wanted to be very well-versed in opera and jazz, which are very important to the movie. I want to be fluent in Italian. And I'm going to take an etiquette class. Anthony said, 'You're pretty virile.' I'm more beer and Ripley is more . . . *delicate*, with the arrogance of an aesthete. I'll lose about twenty pounds for the role."

Damon is quick to say this time around, unlike *Courage Under Fire,* he's going to have the weight lost supervised by a professional.

"I told Anthony, 'I need to do this with a nutritionist,' and he said absolutely. Although, twenty pounds, as opposed to forty-five, is not that bad."

It's a telling commentary on Damon's reputation as an actor that Minghella offered the part to him in the first place, considering the director's take on the actor.

"There's something so apple pie about him. You know he was the best-looking kid in his school and dated the most popular girl."

After *The Talented Mr. Ripley* wraps, Matt has movies lined up almost to the end of the century so although Damon finally bought a house in Los Angeles in the spring of 1998, the odds are he will spend more time away from it than in it.

Among Matt's upcoming projects are the animated sci-fi feature from Fox Family Films, *Planet Ice*.

Set in the future, the Earth has been destroyed by a vicious alien race. Cale (Damon), a nineteen-year-old who has grown up among aliens, finds a map left by his father that reveals a treasure that can save mankind. He teams up with Joe Korso (Bill Pullman) and his crew of renegade aliens and a beautiful pilot (Drew Barrymore) to find Planet Ice and save the Earth.

Then comes *Training Day* opposite Samuel L. Jackson and *All the Pretty Horses*, the film Leonardo DiCaprio was in contract negotiations for, but after it stalled for so long, the producers offered it to Damon instead. The movie is about a cowboy who is wrongly imprisoned and will be directed by *Slingblade*'s Billy Bob Thornton. For his efforts, Damon will be paid $5 million.

And the next collaboration between Matt and Ben, one that will no doubt undergo tremendous scrutiny, is tentatively titled, *Halfway House*, and is about the relationship between two characters in a halfway house, with Damon reportedly playing a patient and Ben a worker.

With all of the work, though, comes a certain responsibility of which Matt himself is acutely aware—he is among the new guard of actors who will lead Hollywood into the new millennium.

"A lot of the male superstars have gotten older and we're having a moment when people in Hollywood are beginning to question who is big right now," points out critic, historian, and Columbia film professor Andrew Sarris.

"They've realized that the $20 million star isn't necessarily a guarantee. A lot of small movies get more and more attention these days and more and more people are going to see those movies. Matt Damon and Ben Affleck didn't have a traditional route to the top."

"These actors seem to want to play interesting characters and tell a great story," says director Richard Linklater, who worked with Ben on *Dazed and Confused*. "I hope this crowd will do what Jack Nicholson did—take one risky role after another and keep taking chances."

It also seems clear that perhaps the time is ripe for an actor like Damon, who prefers to reach an audience through heart rather than special effects.

"We're worn out with action heroes right now," comments Wesleyan University film professor Jeanine Basinger. "Audiences are turning to movies to see their own life reflected. The average moviegoer's life intersects with romance, but it rarely intersects with thundering fireballs and explosions.

"People didn't keep going back to *Titanic* because everyone drowned."

Throughout it all, Damon is determined to keep true to himself and true to his original dream of being the best actor he can be, not the biggest star; that way he will always be able to feel proud of his accomplishments.

"There is never regret at the end of the day, and there won't be with me as long as I know that I did everything I could. If I do everything I can, and people don't like it, I'm still very comfortable talking about it and listening to why it didn't work and getting constructive criticism because this is something I am going to be doing the rest of my life. I'll be doing it in community theater if I have to. This is what I have chosen to do and this is what I am going to do.

"No matter what."